Conversations with Carl: My Journey through Grief

Ethel Erickson Radmer

Conversations with Carl: My Journey through Grief
Copyright © 2006 by Ethel Erickson Radmer

Book Cover Design by Tammy Radmer
Published by Euphonia Publishing, North Carolina
euphoniapublishing@gmail.com
Printed in the USA

ISBN-13: 978-0-9651182-1-7
ISBN-10: 0-9651182-1-5

THANK YOU

Spirit Carl
Your presence in my life is a comfort and joy without bounds.
Your love infuses my existence.

My Grandsons, Asher and Erickson Smith,
Your skillful assistance with computer operations was essential.

Tammy Radmer
Your talent and smarts and love radiated in editing the text
and in designing the front and back covers.

Jane King © 1995
Photograph of Carl Radmer on the horse

Asher Alexander Smith © 2006
Photograph of Ethel Radmer on the beach

CONTENTS

STAGES   Magister Ludi   by Hermann Hesse

As every flower fades and as all youth
Departs, so life at every stage,
So every virtue, so our grasp of truth,
Blooms in its day and may not last forever.
Since life may summon us at every age
Be ready, heart, for parting, new endeavor,
Be ready bravely and without remorse
To find new light that old ties cannot give,
In all beginnings dwells a magic force
For guarding us and helping us to live.
Serenely let us move to distant places
And let no sentiments of home detain us.
The Cosmic Spirit seeks not to restrain us
But lifts us stage by stage to wider spaces.
If we accept a home of our own making,
Familiar habit makes for indolence.
We must prepare for parting and leave-taking
Or else remain the slaves of permanence.
Even the hour of our death may send
Us speeding on to fresh and newer spaces,
And life may summon us to newer races,
So be it, heart: bid farewell without end.

CHAPTER 1
LIFE

"Carl, I don't want to lose you," I softly cried in the middle of the night to my husband, lying next to me at home, and hooked up to an intravenous tube and plastic sac of fluids. Carl had esophageal cancer. Most people with esophageal cancer eventually die of the disease. His survival chances did not look good. I was afraid but I did not want to spread my fear to him.

"You won't lose me," he said in his always kind and confident manner. And I think he believed it at the time. I wanted to believe. I didn't want to think about his not being here.

I loved him so much. We had such a good marriage. We were best friends. Always in tune with each other, I read his thoughts and he mine. We were partners in countless projects, from working together as University of Wisconsin Madison students on advertising campaigns and events to later, in our marriage, building a house addition, foundation up, just the two of us. He could do anything. I had some talents myself and he taught me what I did not know. Together we were a dynamite team, ready to create and construct whatever we desired.

His career was electrical engineering in the world of physics. He was on the team of scientists who designed and built the atomic accelerator at MURA, a consortium of the big Midwestern Universities, in Madison, Wisconsin. They were smashing atoms at incredible speeds to hopefully discover particles of matter that were thought to exist but were not yet actually found. Our family of five lived for two summers on a ranch on a mountaintop in Colorado, while Carl hunted for quarks, one of those illusive particles, conceived of in mathematical formulas but not yet discovered.

Carl continued his connection to atomic accelerators when he moved on to the corporate world. He was one of the top four people who managed a successful electronics company in New York. Besides his scientific expertise, he had an excellent sense of business. He was respected for his brilliance and well liked for the person that he was. As part of his business, Carl frequented other accelerators in the US and especially CERN, the European Center for Nuclear Research, in Geneva, Switzerland. He designed electronics for and worked with Nobel Prize winners in physics and I had the good fortune to meet them also. Carlo Rubbia, an Italian physicist, won the Nobel Prize in physics in 1984 for locating the first W particles and ZO bosons. Rubbia told a colleague once that he had such respect for Carl.

When Asher, our grandson, interviewed Carl for a school project, he wrote about his grandfather. "Something he really cares about is his family. They are important to him because he loves them very much. Something he hopes people will remember about him is that he is a kind and considerate person."

My husband had a fascinating career through all those years and he made a very comfortable living for our family. And we were happy when Carl was able to take an early retirement. We continued to travel to many places in the world. He took on projects of all sorts and told friends, "I wouldn't have time to work now. I am too busy doing other things that I want to do."

I didn't have a better friend. We could talk about anything. He always had smart ideas and suggestions. He had a talent as an engaged, accepting listener. His happiness showed with a winning smile for all. People loved him and I especially did. How fortunate I have been.

We were lovers. He was so attractive, so thoughtful and so sweet. Three children came out of that love, all grown now, with children of their own. Happy, healthy, all of them and doing well. We felt fortunate to have had and to know these great kids.

How could I bear to have this man, my partner in life gone? He was such a huge part of my existence. What a loss it would be to have the father to our children not around. They still seek his guidance. He is a grandfather too, to three grandchildren who love him dearly. They bask in his presence. Such an attentive and caring person he has been with them. They have learned so much from his patient teaching and from his example as a person to emulate. Asher said, "I admire my Grandpa Carl because he has had lots of interesting things happen to him in his life and he was very nice to me." How lucky they have been to have him in their lives. But we all want more years, more time with this special man.

"I'll be around for a long time," he soothed me in our bed. So brave and tender he was. We held each other tightly and we didn't want to let go.

Three months earlier, we had gotten the awful news. At our summer lake house Carl appeared perfectly healthy. He had construction projects to work on and he spent time on the computer with his investments and some writing. He was good at that, too. We hosted family and friends and explored hidden coves of the lake in our motor boat. In late August, out of the blue Carl leapt up from the dinner table and ran outside. He admitted later to our guests and to me that his food had suddenly come up. Later in bed, Carl and I puzzled over what had happened and we weren't too alarmed. We decided to return to North Carolina and our apartment to see a doctor there and find out what was wrong.

We went straight to a gastroenterologist, knowing that something was happening in his GI tract where food travels. On the spot, the doctor did an esophageal endoscopy. Carl was sedated and a tube with a camera and light on the end was put down his throat. They saw a tumor growing from the wall into the opening of the esophagus at the distal part of the throat, where the sphincter at the stomach was not closing like it should be doing. Acid reflux, coming from the stomach through the opening, caused Barrett esophagus, a changing of the cells that were lining his throat. That in turn over time can lead to cancer. He also had barium swallow X-rays, a CAT scan, dilation of the obstructed area, and a biopsy.

Later, the doctor gave Carl and me his diagnosis. Carl had adenocarcinoma in the bottom of his esophagus. A cancerous mass was blocking the passage for food and water. It was a shocking report but we took the news amazingly calmly. We asked questions, talked about chemotherapy, radiation, and alternative treatments and we were out the door.

Quietly leaving the building, hand in precious hand, I offered, "Carl, I am so at peace." "So am I," he returned, with a gentle caress of his palm on mine. It was an amazing thing to receive that diagnosis and to feel a sense of peace. I don't know where that feeling of calm came from but we rose to the occasion.

Carl and I really thought he was going to make it, be well and beat the odds. Then we could get on with our lives. Carl wrote in a three-page open letter to friends and family that fall, "I and Ethel are in the best of spirits, and we intend to keep it that way. We are truly happy, making this into an adventure."

In December he wrote in another open letter, "The other week grandson Asher made a cute giraffe out of foam, with a label that says his name is Tanzania. The Get Well Giraffe, and a blobby thing that he labeled The Dead Cancer Germ, both are on my computer desk shelf in my line of sight, like little idols for me to honor." Carl signed off with, "We are still, very positive, optimistic and convinced that this will do it. So far, things are going well. Life is great, I expect to be around for a long time in order to keep enjoying it. With best regards, and love for all – Carl."

We did have four precious months together. We were alive! We lived fully like we always did. We loved as lovers could and would. We walked on the Greenway paths near our apartment. We drove to Duke Gardens, which was resplendent in fall colors. We walked the garden paths and sat dreamily on a bench, always holding hands. At the lily pond there was a tree inviting us to climb. Carl could reach the first limb easily but I could not. So Carl boosted me up and we sat on the sturdy limb close together and gazed at the weeping willow tree nearby with its long curved branches gracefully hanging over the water. It was shedding tears for us with its morning dew. We didn't talk. Our time was too precious to speak. Quiet soothed our kindred souls.

Carl planned a trip. We needed to get away from the treatments and get a fresh view. So on a weekend, we drove to the Great Smokey Mountains. They are among the oldest mountains in the world, perhaps 200-300 million years ago. Their awesome age dwarfs our life span. Holding each other's hands, we walked to a high point and saw in the distance the peak of Mount Mitchell, rising more than a mile high, the highest mountain in the Appalachian Mountain range. The gentle mist of the low-hanging clouds was a tonic to our weary selves. The weight of our concerns was lightened with seeing nature's remarkable creation.

Back home, we took our grandsons to the playground. We pushed Asher and Eric on the swings. Carl joined the boys on the rocking horses.

We all slid down the slides and called out "wheeeee!" in the fun. Ah, to be a child again!

Our San Francisco kids visited. Randy came to have a long weekend with his Dad. They talked like they always talked. Science and plans and everyday happenings. I casually took a picture of them sitting on swivel chairs and smiling at each other and wondered to myself if this might be their last time together. Tammy and Dave flew in for Thanksgiving. Such gladness and love and good cheer we shared together. All of us gave thanks that Carl could be eating a meal with us. Carl exuded happiness.

I cleaned out my writing files. I had a dozen books to be born in those files and I tossed them out. It seemed a rash thing to do but the unsettling happenings that had befallen our contented lives must have set the stage for me to clear out my life. Bag after bag of papers I carried to the dumpster. Carl saw me shedding the past years. "Carl," I said that fall, "I feel like I am getting ready for my death." Carl didn't say anything.

Was that tossing out a metaphor for my death to come? The passing of my self as I was with Carl? To the different person, without Carl, I would become?

One morning when we awoke in bed, Carl told me about a dream he had in the night. He rarely mentioned his dreams. Alarm was in his voice. The story was so poignant, so ominous. But the content of the dream wasn't registering with me. I was too afraid. It just passed through my anxious brain. I could only feel his fear and my own alarm with his fear. The story seemed to warn us of something that was to come. We lay close and I just moaned, "Oh, Carl."

The radiation and chemotherapy were taking their toll. His throat was raw and full of sores. He was weaker. But in the Christmas 1996 photo of our family, Carl and I with our children, their spouses and our grandkids one last sweet time, Carl stood tall, looking the picture of health, with his always-effervescent smile. It was eleven days before his death.

Pneumonia probably from the radiation passing through Carl's chest put him in the hospital just days after our Christmas together. The children returned from the West to be together again.

Carl's radiation oncologist told us that Carl Sagan, the famous astronomer had just died on December 20th He felt a big loss and Carl and I did too. The similar circumstances between Carl and Carl were surprising, besides their names and their radiant smiles. Sagan died of pneumonia from other complications. He had been on chemotherapy and radiation as Carl had been. They were both sixty-two years of age, born within a week of each other and died two weeks apart. I used to call Carl the Carl Sagan of physics. Carl Radmer, though not famous, was so clear and engaging when speaking to a large group or conversing one on one with people about the complexities and intricacies of the physics world. He helped to make sense of the invisible components and forces in the minutest form of matter. Carl Sagan was mesmerizing when he talked on television to millions of watchers about the 'billions and billions' of stars. We have the miniscule components of matter in contrast to the vastness of space. Astronomy quests for the infinitely big. Physics searches for the infinitesimally small. Both are trying to solve the mysteries of our existence.

Even while Carl was in the hospital, our children and I hoped that he would make it through this and be well. But the last couple of days up to January fifth, we all knew that in the mysteries of our existence, Carl, our beautiful man, so worthy of more life on this earth, was probably going to die.

In Carl's last days alive, I sat on his bed, close up to him and said, "I love you." As I lifted his oxygen mask, he softly said, "I love you." He looked intently at me. The corners of my mouth started going down as I felt so sad and choked up. He reached over with his right hand and with his thumb and index finger he raised the sides of my mouth into a smile. Then he smiled through his mask and gave me a wink with his right eye. It makes me weep as I am writing this.

Oh, dear, dear man. You have embraced me with your heart. "Be happy," you are saying without words. "Be happy. Life goes on."

CHAPTER 2
MOURNING

Dear Carl, my lover, my best friend, my husband for almost thirty-nine years. Can you hear me? With every spark of energy I have I want to believe that you are there. I hoped for a sign, like we had spoken of a couple of months before you died, not expecting you would die. We came up with no sign and you said then that it might not work. That's not to say you didn't believe part of you or maybe, more encompassing, the whole of you, beyond what we see in earthly form, would live on. In your letter to our children at Christmas that we enclosed in the books we gave them, eleven days before you died, you expressed yourself with candor.

"I do believe that we are all spirits, or souls, or actually part or extensions of one multi-dimensional Great Spirit (I call it/us the Great Oneness, Of Which I Am Part) living temporarily in a limited 3-dimensional body here on earth. While here we are veiled from seeing much of that spiritual part of us, some folks more than others."

You evolved so beautifully in your beliefs through the years, but especially through the four months that you knew you had cancer. You confronted death head on, so courageously, and at the same time thought you would make it - we both passionately thought you would - and would be rid of the unwelcome growth in your body.

You also said in your letter to our children, daringly from a scientist, "I also believe that we (our spirits) are here (on earth) to learn, a sort of grad school for spirits, and that we have probably been here many times (previous lives) and will come probably back many times. Each 'life lesson' usually elevates the spirit to a slightly higher plane, with the goal being the Buddhist's "nirvana."

My belief in our souls living on was not quite as certain as yours was. I was more on the cusp, wanting it so much to be so but wishing for a hint of evidence. The reverse of what you would think it might be - you the scientist and me the artist. But your engineering, logical mind saw the sense of our energy transforming and departing the earth for another realm. And I, who am left behind (does that "behind" say I really do believe in the afterlife?), imagining the beauty and the music of continuing our path beyond, want my sight, sound, feel senses to confirm it.

And now you are gone. If wishing made it so, I would have your spirit right here with me. I do feel you here, I definitely feel your presence, but I think it is what we had in the past and it continues. How could you who were such a huge chunk of my life not be part of me now and for time to come?

Carl, I miss you. As happy as I want to be, as I was together with you, as I know you would want me to be now, I felt a gaping hole with your death. My balance was thrown to the winds. My rhythms and patterns were shaken to the core. How cavalier we were to say to each other at least a year ago that if one of us 'went' the other one of us would manage. It's true - you do manage - but the shock for me is much greater than we imagined. The reality of your death was so strong, magnified to strengths beyond what I thought I could take in. I was not numbed as I have heard so many people say they are in early grief. My senses were intensified, livened to greater increments. And somehow I did manage to take it all in.

Our children were all with you when you died. Our grandsons, had their last tender touching moments with you just days before you died and you held them in your arms and loved them so. They came again right after you died and touched your tanned, long arms and laid their heads on your chest. Through their tears, they softly cried, "I love you Grandpa Carl." What a grandpa you were with them. The car trips you made with each one alone, across the country to New Mexico with Eric and up and down the East Coast with Asher. Those were adventures they'll talk about for years to come. You built wooden toys with them. You made up dozens of bedtime stories that you told them through the years. They are stored in beyond price banks of memories. What a gift that was for all three of you.

We watched for hours on that last day while you were giving in to the struggle for your breath. It was then that we knew you were going to die. I lay on the bed alongside you, my right hand gently touching your heaving chest, as I had done on previous days, my head against yours and whispered longingly in your ear. "I love you. I love you. I don't want to lose you. You are a wonderful person. Be well." Our children, through six days of your hospital stay, had loved you and talked with you. The girls played crossword puzzles with you like you all used to do, while they nibbled on the food brought to you that you could not eat. They all made their peace with you, while hoping and almost expecting you would live. But your last breath came on a quarter to noon, Sunday. We watched you die.

The oxygen tank kept swooshing bizarrely after you took your last weak breath; oblivious to you and us, through the mask we took gently from your face. I had lifted that mask several times to kiss you throughout the week and now it was not needed, cast aside with the oxygen still pumping through. Trying still to give you life, even after your life had left your beautiful body.

Teri, Randy, Tammy, David, Asher, Erickson all said their good-byes to you with loving tears and kisses. Touching you, crying over your quiet body. Did your spirit hear our plaintive cries or feel our desolation?

The children left for home but I wanted to stay longer with you alone. I gently embraced almost every inch of your body with my hands. It was cool now. It was so beautiful as in life. I cried. I called to you. To your spirit, wondering if it was there. Longing to feel that a part of you lived on. You were quiet. I looked and listened. I touched the air but felt nothing. I could only imagine your soul lifting up and leaving for a higher plane. And if anyone deserved a higher plane, you did. You were so loving, kind, giving. Your wonderful smile in life embraced us all and still does.

I don't know how long I stayed with you, but after some length of time, I felt it was time to go. "Goodbye darling Carl," I said aloud, choked with tears. While slowly making my way to your door and looking back a last time at your silent form, I blew you a kiss and left you alone. Alone too, I drove home, feeling my mind in a still-frame. It was locked on "Carl is dead." What we did not expect happened. What we hoped against hope for was not to be.

Our children and grandsons were waiting for me in our apartment. Loving looks. Concern for my trip alone. Talking quietly. The boys doing art work to channel their sorrow. Carl, you would have been touched with Asher's miniature 3 dimensional paper creation, an exact joyful likeness of you in your favorite yellow shirt, the top half of you showing in a sailboat, your smiling face directly in the wind. You are so alive! Erickson made a color drawing of you in your car. It's a loving remembrance of your travels together.

They asked me, "What are you going to do now, Grandma Ethel? Are you still going to move to California?" "Yes, I still want to go, partly to honor Grandpa, since we planned to do that together. I want to have time with our family there. And I want to go on a retreat. I want to be alone with my thoughts."

I asked everyone to take what each wanted of Carl's mementos, his clothes, and the few possessions he had left. Carl and I had simplified our lives with our moves and pared down to basic needs. In past years, we had given away our art collection, my black ebony Baldwin baby grand piano, many of our clothes and books, most of our furniture, all our antiques, and anything else filling up a space. So there was not much left. They each took what they wanted and the clothes that were left went into a couple of boxes ready to ship to special people. I saved out two things for myself to keep for awhile, a charcoal gray wool sweater and a blue bathrobe that Carl always wore. I wanted to feel and smell and touch the essence of him in the fiber next to my skin.

We stayed together for hours in the library, listening to the CD you and I bought together at Christmas, our last. 'A Musical Voyage,' serene, dreamy music that had us floating on clouds with our private memories and sadness. I wanted to take that musical voyage with you and the California voyage and many other voyages to come. And you are on your own voyage now if what you believed is true. It's comforting, the thought of it.

We talked about you. Were your ears ringing?

CHAPTER 3
MOVING

Hey Carl, here's my variation on John Denver's song. 'Leaving On A Jet Plane.'

'All my bags are packed. I'm ready to go.....So kiss me and smile for me. Tell me that you'll stay with me. Hold me like you'll never let me go…Cause I'm leavin' North Carolina on a jet plane. Don't know when I'll be back again…Oh, babe, I love you so. Cause I'm leavin' North Carolina on a jet plane. And I won't be back again.'

I won't be back to my former self, that is. I'll never bc the same. Please Spirit Carl, stay with me wherever I go. Keep your smiles coming. And give me as much holding as you can manage. Who knows what lies ahead for me in new places? I'd like company. Your spirit could comfort a lonely heart. Your smile might quench a barren soul. If I free fall, please catch and hold me tight. And Honey, I love you so.

After your death, my spirit or was it yours, drew me to special places we had been before you died. I revisited Duke Gardens. The bench was so lonely without you and my eyes filled up with tears. I looked at the tree we climbed and wondered how I could get up to that limb without your helping hand. I looked and looked and figured out a way. I did it! Carl, you would be so pleased and happy for me! I sat on that limb and thought. This is a metaphor for my life to come. If I can't do it I'll find a way. Whatever might stop me or block me, I can get through it. I can manage without you, my dear, at least this one time.

The Greenway paths called me back to our last sharing of nature's beauty. I returned to the bookstore where I had given a talk about the book I wrote, "The Cheshire Cat Syndrome: My Adventures With Arthritis." You had started your cancer treatment then but you were with me and gave me your attentive support. We last shopped there at Christmas for our CD and the children's books. I remembered the aisles that we walked, the normalcy of our errands, the clothes you wore.

Our dear New York friends, Harriet Cornell and Jane King planned a memorial service for you a month after you died. It was in Upper Nyack in one of those lovely old mansions on the Hudson River that we occasionally had reason to visit. The many tributes to you were beautiful, heartfelt and touching. You should feel honored to be held in such high esteem. Our dear friend Gene told a wonderful story of our camping trips together and said in the middle of it, "Being with Carl was experiencing a great sense of peace. He had such a quiet and profound sweetness about him that he restored my faith in humanity." Deandra, one of Teri's best friends, stood in front of the group and tearfully said that she didn't really have a father in her life and that you were like a father to her. I tried to talk to the group and got all choked up.

It has been just two months since your death and I am flying away. Teri and I have been on the computer, on the phone and in people's offices starting to settle your estate. The job is more manageable now.

Teri and David and the children have been a comforting presence in my life. I will miss them. The apartment is lonely without you. I have packed up my things. I am ready to move on, as I told Asher and Eric I would do

Against all conventional wisdom to stay put in early grief, I am leaving the familiar and the comfortable behind me. I am starting over. People do get second chances. Across the country I am flying to create a whole new life for myself.

But you, my dear, are not surprised. We have spent a lot of time in the air to get to unfamiliar thereabouts and whereabouts. We are adventurous spirits, part of our attraction when we first met. There are new things to discover and our time on this earth doesn't last forever, witness your demise. I am on my own adventure, now.

California, here I come! My seatmate on this small plane is a pilot, though he's a passenger on this flight. He informs me that Fort Funston, California, where the hang gliders fly, is right below us. I lean past him to look out, as the plane lowers altitude to land just north at the San Francisco Airport.

I see one! The hang glider is just a mark in the sky. Flying so freely, floating where the wind blows, head on into the sky. Over the ocean he weaves and on up the coast. It could be you, Carl. You're a pilot. But I see me! I want to do that! How brave that would be.

One of the sympathy cards that I received and treasure shows two distant eagles flying in the sky and a message, "May your cares fall like feathers from the wings of eagles as you fly strong and free toward the sun." It is packed in my bags.

I see another metaphor for my new life, honey. Sailing into the unknown. Strong and free. I have no baggage – thank God and thanks to such a happy life with you. I want to fill my senses with the new.

We land and Randy, my son, meets me. How glad I am to see him. I feel a little shaky. Maybe I'm not so brave, after all. But family warmth embraces me and I'm glad to be home. My new home is San Francisco. Home of the brave and the free. That is me.

Randy and Bonnie and Lauren are hosting me for a couple of weeks until my apartment is ready to move into. They have helped me with so many things. Randy has taken me places, made connections for me and helped to set up my apartment. I am so grateful. Tammy and Dave have helped me become reacquainted with the Bay area.

So I haven't been totally alone, Carl. They have greased the skids. Our caring for each other is a comfort. We share a loss. You are terribly missed by all of us.

And now I am alone. I have moved into my own space. It is my first place without you in thirty-nine years. The apartment suits me well and I am ready to explore the surrounding turf on my own terms.

I catch the sail or take the plunge. This city is a potpourri of offerings, full of things to see and do. Remembering from past times here, I have so much to take in. The first thing is the charm. Who can resist the charm? Carl, I'm falling in love with a city! You know what

I mean!

I have made the right move to the West. I feel it. It seems radical to others to leave the comfort of home and a support system of family and friends, but this is just what I need for a shaken-up psyche and a lonely heart. Having put my toes in the water and knowing I have a clear stage for my new life, I am ready for retreat. Now, I want to explore my heart.

CHAPTER 4
RETREAT

It seems, the more strongly I want you, looking for signs and signals from you, the cloudier is the connection. At the New Camaldoli Hermitage I am in quiet retreat, nestled in the Santa Lucia Mountains in the region of Big Sur and I find myself wanting you almost desperately. I feel the missing so strongly that I think it overloads the neural connections in my brain, it oozes into all my spaces, and the clarity of your presence is gone. Soft, far-away thoughts from you drift in my brain – "I know." "Yes." "Sleep." But, it's as if you are on some distant shore. You're not available. I sense that you are learning about a new place, like I have done in San Francisco, and you are finding your own place in it. Your attention is not on earthly things. Carl, I understand.

I am in my own place, a place of seclusion. I told Asher and Eric on the day you died, feeling that you heard it, that I wanted to go on a retreat and think my own thoughts. And here I am. In the privacy of my reflections, withdrawn from the full life I am making for myself in the city. I am in solitude. In isolation in my cell – yes it is called a cell. In silence I sit in my private garden, with foxes present, atop the mountain. The beach and the ocean below are spread out magnificently in a curve, so broad and far out is the azure blue. There is no end to the sky. It is in my interregnum, between your death and whenever I will feel whole again, in my present isolation from distractions, that with irony, I feel, more than ever before, connected to the vastness of the universe.

I want to believe that you are there, somewhere, in some form. But, this skeptic is not sure. I can imagine it and feel it and even hear your thoughts in my head, but I can't quite surrender to the absoluteness of it. You know, Carl, I am a hard nut to crack.

The monks' life suits me, though I'm not a monk of this Benedictine Order. I'm neither male nor under religious orders. But, I am living apart, as a monk does, albeit a short while, from many parts of my life. I go to the chapel to hear the monks chant and to see the rituals, several times a day. The monks sing the liturgy at Vigils, Lauds, mass, and Vespers. After Vespers we have a silent meditation. I'm not a Catholic by any means, you know both of us, and I'm not looking to be one. But I find the ceremony and the monks comforting. Meditating with others in the church rotunda is powerful in the stillness. There is such peace here. The spare food agrees with me, too. Simple salad, vegetarian soup and bread freshly made by the monks are left in a small pantry. I serve myself and eat in my cell alone and in silence.

This monastery, thirteen hundred feet above the sea, is grounded on a contemplative and eremitical lifestyle espoused by Saint Romuald, its founder. "Sit in your cell as in paradise. Put the whole world behind you and forget it," the good saint advised. "Watch your thoughts like a good fisherman watching for fish."

My favorite monk – is it sacrilegious to have favorites? – is

Brother Isaiah. He met me in the bookstore when I arrived, the one place to talk, quietly of course, and he has shown me kindness in chapel and on the walking paths. His appearance helps too. With a full dark beard, he looks like he belongs on a Smith Brothers' cough drop box. I have arranged to have talks with him in a room off the bookstore.

Brother Isaiah is so full of Christian charity as I sit in the rocking chair and he sits in a straight one. He emanates love as I share my story about you dear Carl, our kids, my sadness, my wishing to be fully happy. He's a good listener, Carl, like you, and I feel comfortable to shed tears and show my pain.

I told Brother Isaiah that one thing I would want us to do if we could replay our last four months together would be to discuss death openly. Carl, my love, we did not talk death. We barely touched it. I think because we were both so sure you were going to make it and somehow I think we both felt it would interfere with the optimistic, positive, "expect only wellness" trip we were on. It is one of those things that brings me tears - tears for our bravery and tears for what we might have shared. Brother Isaiah suggested that I write down what I would have wished we had spoken of in a dialogue.

Ethel: Carl, I want to broach the subject of death with you. It's a possibility for either one of us. We both think that you are going to get through this cancer and yet. What if you do die? Let's face the chance of it, even though we think you will beat the odds.

Carl: It could happen. We all die eventually and it could be in the next months or year or years in my case. Or maybe it will be decades from now.

Ethel: Oh, I so want that to be true. I don't want to lose you. But Carl, If we knew that one of us was going to die what would we want to say to the other?

Carl: If I die, it's just a passing. My spirit, soul, call it what you will, will be on some level of awareness out there. And you will do fine without me. You can certainly take care of yourself. You are capable, smart. You can figure things out. You have friends and family. There's love there. You're healthy. You do good things to take care of yourself. You're youthful and active.

Ethel: I love you.

Carl: I love you too, very much.

Ethel: I don't want to lose you.

Carl: You won't. I'll be here for a long time.

Ethel: What about the practical things? Like money?

Carl: You have plenty of money. You have more money than if I were alive, both of us living off of it.

Ethel: But you are here to manage it. You love to sit at the computer and buy stock, go to the library and look at Morningstar, bring up possible investments with me, discuss it and we decide together. But you are the smarts, you care about it with a passion. I am happy to just know that I have enough to pay for the rent, food, health needs, travel, and satiating my mind with books, music, art, studies, and writing. I don't want to be doing what you're doing.

Carl: Sell the stock. Buy mutual funds. Put money in money market as you need to live off of. You'll get social security after I die. You have some life insurance off of me. Keep up your health insurance with the company.

Ethel: But now in our really facing death, Carl, what would you add in your advice to me on managing money? In a nutshell?

Carl: Have fun with it. Be glad you have money. Don't worry about it. Go to the library and find good mutual funds. Do what you want with it. I won't be here so what does it matter to me?

Ethel: That's hard for me to imagine! You care a lot about what happens to your money now. I have trouble seeing that you wouldn't wince with an investment that loses money or groan with the stock value going down, even after death. Wow! That's suddenly looking like proof to me of the afterlife! What a kick! That the one thing that convinces me that our souls live on is that I can't imagine that you wouldn't have, even after death, strong reactions to money matters!

Carl: I wouldn't be here so what do I care.

Ethel: Carl, I have been so dependent on you for the computer. Granted, I can spend hours, hitting keys on the keyboard alone, no one the wiser. Then I have a hitch that I can't solve and I call for you. You are there or will be there in hours and you bail me out. It's a dependency I wish I didn't have and you are so sweet about. You give, you are available, you fix it, and you are just there with only kindness. Carl, I don't want to give that up. It shows your nature so well, your gifts of love.

Carl: You have fixed things. You've solved problems. You'll be able to figure out what to do. And if you can't you can ask someone.

Ethel: That is what I love about you. You are so matter of fact. You make it sound so possible, so doable. You have faith, trust, confidence, and love.

Carl: I do what I can.

Ethel: What do you think about dying, Carl? Months before we had any idea of your cancer with its attendant death-knell, you said in conversations that death didn't scare you. When the time comes, you would be ready to die. That you have lived a good, full life and that death happens. And I admitted to you that I didn't feel quite as accepting as you of death and wished I had reached your level of acquiescence. Now that we are facing death more squarely I want to pour my heart out to you. Carl, I love you so much, I just want you here, I want our lives to go on together. Together we are so rich in feelings, fun, energy, plans. We're so in sync. I can't imagine that with anyone else and that isn't my concern anyway. I just want you! I'm crying because I don't want you to go.

Carl: I'm smiling, Ethel, because you will be fine. You can enjoy life without me. I want you to have a great life.

Ethel: Oh, Carl. That is just too sweet. You are always thinking of me - with absolute love and confidence. And how would you feel if

I died before you?

Carl: I would miss you a lot. I would want you back. And I would get used to it. I would be glad for all we had and enjoy the new life I would have.

Ethel: Carl, I've said similar things before but I want to say again, this time letting show to you my heart bursting. I admire with awe your positivism and your determination to get well. If anyone should and could get well it would be you. You are the one for people to emulate.

Carl: I AM proud of how I've been able to feel about this. And you are a reason and perhaps the reason for my feeling this way. We are so together.

Ethel: Carl, what if you don't get over the cancer? Would you wish we had done something differently?

Carl: Oh, I might think that briefly, but I truly feel we did our best and I have no regrets. You helped me so much in what I did and how I feel. And wasn't it a great ride?

Ethel: I want to be happy and I am all choked up. With our love for each other, with all the good things, with the exquisite person you are.

Carl: Thank you. But, I'm not perfect.

Ethel: Well, close to perfect.

That is so you, Carl. It's just what you would have said or did say snippets of when we were together. Thank you for the good advice.

I did feel it was Carl talking through me. The suggestions that he gave me are just what he would have given in life. His sweet words came through so quickly, as if he were still alive, conversing happily with me.

On the mountain above the ocean, I explored my heart and found it rich with feelings. They poured forth in a fount of tears. Brother Isaiah was my confidant, my consoler, and a spirit of grace to my heart in need. His peace, like the dove, filled my being.

As Saint Romuald advised, I sat in my monk's cell as in paradise. I sobbed and cried my heart out and somehow there was beauty in the overflow. It's possible, I think, that there are tears in heaven. It completes our essence. We are fully God's creation in the lamentation.

My earthly world with you celestial Carl, is behind us. My elegy of tears made that fact real. But parting from Saint Romuald's counsel to forget, I will summon up my keepsake of precious memories from time to time.

Romuald said to watch your thoughts like a good fisherman watching for fish. And perhaps that is what I did. Midst all the mourning I captured illusive thoughts of happiness and of a tasty course ahead.

CHAPTER 5
COMFORT

Comfort, Carl. I want comfort in my grief! I am crying and I am trying to reach your spirit. With every part of my being, I wish for, I long for comfort. I want to be held and soothed, Carl, my love, and to be given love. You would have given that to me. That's the irony. I need you alive to give me what I most want with your death.

Our children have their own grief burden to bear, their own shakiness and sadness. I know it weighs heavily on them. They don't have the emotional strength to deal with mine. Glimpses come through. Tammy has shown me around special places in San Francisco, including where the hang-gliders take off and land! But, remember, Carl, she is pregnant and the hormones are raging. She has a Herculean task to keep from tipping her psyche and her body.

Randy, who has been so helpful to me, finding my apartment, talking for hours about practical things and investments, has even said he thinks a lot about my being alone and it makes him feel sad. But, Randy is in pain. I know it. He keeps it hidden like he keeps himself buried in his home office research.

Teri's Asher, just eleven years, so missing you, his dear Grandpa Carl, called me on the phone in tears with his sadness. It's so good that he could do that. I felt touched with his reaching out to me. Erickson, ten years, is all tied up inside himself with his grief. He loved you so much. You built wooden toys with him that had moving parts. He'll treasure those memories, but he is so sad.

Teri is giving lengths of time with business matters and helping to settle an estate. And she is pregnant, too, you were happy to know. Two boys already and earning an advanced degree. A lot to handle. She and I have managed to laugh - about your ashes - a week after you died, resting in the breakfront right next to our chairs. "We almost forgot!" "Oh, you're there!" "Carl, you're trapped in a box!" "With all due respect, we are not being very respectful, we know!"

They have all been a support in their own way, doing the best they can in tough times. Friends have called and written. They are missing you, too. You were so loved.

That has helped me, but it's a thick skin this grief. I can't seem to shed it. I make openings for happiness and have wonderful moments with family, beauty, hiking, books, but the nagging weight is often there. Oh, to be lighter!

Feeling on my own with this grief thing, I searched for grief groups. Not eagerly, because I'm wary of people being totally self-centered with their sadness. I eagerly extend myself to the world around me and some people can't seem to move outside their own heads. But I'd like to try meeting others who share this experience of loss. Talking with them might have some benefits.

Talking with a therapist, though, does not interest me. I'm sure they are a godsend for many people but I don't want to shop around for just the right one. What I would want from a professional is total acceptance, genuine caring, no judging, no telling me what to do, no sticking me in psychiatric slots, no stooping to 'what a tragedy.' I would want a listener with heart and if words come out, let them be kind. That's a tall order. If the order is not met, I'm afraid there might be damage to my sometimes, fragile psyche. Let's not add insult to injury. I'm already bruised with my loss. I'm much safer without their help.

Grief groups are tough to track down. There seems to be no central network, at least at the time that I was hunting. I tried the University of California Medical Center up the hill, various hospitals, social service agencies and churches. One phone call led to another and to another and eventually I found two promising groups. I tried both.

The Jewish Center had a grief support group across the street from Mount Zion Hospital. There were four of us plus a leader at a Tuesday afternoon gathering. I wore a gray wool business jacket over a knit top, with black slacks and I looked clean-cut and unimposing. I wanted to show my serious intent and my respect for all the participants as well as for the deceased. Carl, your powerful presence in my head and dare I say, my aura, made me feel strong. I had no desire to weep, though I sympathized with the others. People need to release their sadness. Their tears flowed and their barely audible, choked up words spilled out from all three. They were totally caught up in themselves, with no energy left to extend out. I listened and responded with kind words to all. The leader was calm and cool and had her agenda of stages to know in the grief process. I'm sure that is very helpful to many, but I am not into setting up steps and stages in any emotional process. The journey is so different for everyone! 'Steps' ring of expectations and what is 'normal,' which do not serve as a useful guide for me and only throw me off my own track and trip. I don't want preconceived notions influencing my steps. I gave it the "old college try' twice more, just in case it might prove helpful. The usefulness was in my realizing that I am at a different place than the others and that I am a wayfarer on my own pilgrimage

I tried a group once again, this time with the widow/widowers group at the Visiting Nurse Hospice on Geary Boulevard. It was a much larger group. One man dominated the time and others wanted to talk. The facilitator did not intervene so I did. Gently, I told him that another woman had something to say. Again these people were in deep grief. I am in grief too, but I felt no comfort here.

When I felt bereft without you before the Thanksgiving and Christmas holidays I joined the Salvation Army Corps of volunteers and delivered meals to needy people in the Tenderloin, a drug-ridden and unsafe area of the city. I learned a lot about the seamy side of life. It did not raise my spirits or comfort my soul, but I felt very grateful for my own life.

Carl, my clearheaded friend, I have come to this realization. There is no one to comfort me but myself. I am the one. No one can take away my pain, no matter how much they would wish it. I, Ethel, am able to take it away myself, in my own head and heart, and I am working on it.

Talking to you helps, because, with the quiet of my closeness to you, the feelings surge. There's no repression here. I'm attentive to whatever message or signals you might have to show.

And here's the tough part. I am trying to accept reality. How can I have been clearheaded about practically everything in my life and yours and in your death have trouble accepting the reality of it? I hope it comes with time.

Here is my comfort. Early this morning in bed, I felt your presence strongly and welcomed your words, every single word.

"I love you very much. I wanted to stay with you, but I left. You are doing fine. I'm proud of you. I really want you to be happy. Enjoy life. Get as much out of life as you can. If you feel bad about anything and wished you had done some things differently, don't feel bad. It's ok. It's fine. I'm here and you're there. Have a good time. Love life. We truly did the best we could together and loved each other for it."

Carl, what you say is a gift. I am seeing this jolt of your passing and the incumbant sadness I have felt, as an opportunity to explore all my beliefs and maybe uncover stuff I didn't even know was there that might contribute to any down feeling. I am learning a lot about myself. I want to find what might be getting in the way of my full happiness. I'm really evaluating and evolving my thinking and behavior. Questioning my beliefs and then I can change them if they don't serve me. I'm doing it! You and I did this in your living state, going from being happy to being even happier. Asking, "What am I feeling? Why? Uncovering a belief. Asking why I believe that." It worked for us and it is slowly working for me.

I'm trying to always be a loving person to others because it feels good and to exude kindness because I like being kind and to be giving because it helps with the grief. You certainly were loving and kind and giving. Is it your legacy that I'm trying to emulate and perpetuate? Somehow, this shaking up of my psyche with your death, has given me a chance to be even better, more fulfilled, to be even more peaceful, and even glowing inside and out. I like that! Why shouldn't I be even happier than ever? The grief pundits may laugh at that, but I know you would applaud.

This evening I attended a Greek Tragedy seminar downtown that I take from my friend Dr. Hal Sarf. I said that maybe the 'fallacy' of crazy thinking - does grief qualify as crazy thinking? - be it Greek gods or humans, was that some of us are crazy when in fact we're all crazy - a little. Tom, one of the guys in the seminar, said that what we need in our craziness is just talking, talking, talking, and not therapy. But we don't have anyone to talk with except our therapist for 50 minutes for $90. His comments reminded me of needing to talk out my own grief. Brother Isaiah at the Hermitage was so accepting as a listener. And you are, my love, my perfect mate in my grief, all unto yourself and myself, the par excellence of 'being with,' a spirit without walls, available and open. Thank you Carl for listening.

CHAPTER 6
ANEW

The joys of this city are boundless! I am zipping, dipping, flipping around, into, and over so many good things. The landscape, the book talks, the libraries, the University of California San Francisco lectures, the art, the music, the dance. I am full with the beauty and excitement. And our kids live here! We see a lot of each other. What a treat this all is.

The geological wonders abound. I can walk in the park or stay put in my apartment and take it all in. Out my window I see the rolling hills of San Francisco, the big solid green patch of Golden Gate Park, the rolling green acres of eucalyptus in the Presidio and, just beyond the Bay, the rounded hills of the Marin headlands. The Golden Gate Bridge, connecting the city to Marin County, shines red copper in the sunlight. What a glorious sight it is looking out or standing on my deck. And I know there is so much beyond. I've already explored in past years or want to soon the endless coast, the Sierra Mountains, the charm of Mendocino.

The offerings for the mind, I soak up ravenously. Book talks abound with famous authors. Feminist authors frequent this liberal city. I've heard several of them. Gloria Steinem a couple of times and Naomi Wolf promoting her book Promiscuities. I met Robert Thurman, the founder of Tibet House, twice, and I heard Paul Thoreaux at Stanford University. I've read most of his books. Dave and I went to the Haight, had dinner, and heard Dan Millman talk about The Peaceful Warrior. Carl, you and I read the book, 'Secret of the Peaceful Warrior,' to our grandsons several times and it taught good lessons, teaching conflict resolution as a peaceful warrior, not by fighting or by running away, but by facing your fears.

I take in lectures at the University of California Medical, thanks to Randy who earned his PhD there and put me on to it, on every medical subject. Dr. Dean Ornish, on the faculty, speaks about his low fat diet regimen for heart patients. There are many lectures on alternative approaches to health. It didn't keep you alive, dear Carl, but the subject is dear to my heart. Naturopathic medicine, acupuncture, and pranic healing are just a few.

I've spent time at many of the public libraries, if not most, including the Chinese Library. Yes, I love books and the spaces that they occupy. I joined the Mechanics Institute Library, a private library downtown, for really old texts and stimulating talks and for comfortable hanging out.

Carl, I'm back in your milieu! The physics world attracted me like atomic and subatomic particles are pulled in a cyclotron's magnetic field. The University of San Francisco has a weekly physics colloquium. I've walked across the park many times to the campus to hear physicists, some of whom are Nobel Prize winners. I wonder each time if you mixed with any of them. One talk was 'Trapping Atoms with Light.' I like the concept from an aesthetic point of view as well as the scientific. Nobel winner Douglas Osheroff from Stanford spoke on 'Super Fluidity in 3Helium.' He's known as a low temperature physicist. You, Carl, operated in the high energy physics world so you probably would not have spent time in another special area of physics. SETI people have come to report on progress in the search for extra-terrestrial intelligence. We go from the miniscule to the vastness of space! I like learning about current thinking and research and I feel a connection with you that you might not have expected that I would have in your death.

I frequent Golden Gate Park with its museums for art and science as well as the Arboretum and Stow Lake. I go with family or friends or by myself. These attractions and a lot more are all just down the hill from where I live - alone.

I wish you were here. But, you know what? I feel it's my life to create. I am like the artist that I am, ready with all senses open, looking at an almost limitless, unmarked canvas, holding a palette of incredible colors. I can create whatever I wish.

Today, I took the N Judah train, as I've done many times these months, from the Inner Sunset District to Market Street downtown and walked to Nordstrom's. Later I would meet my friend Elizabeth for dinner and, with time to myself, I followed the sound of the grand piano to the fourth level. I sat in a stuffed chair off to the side of the pianist. He played beautifully. His fingers raced nimbly up and down the keyboard with familiar tunes and composers. Gershwin, Cole Porter. I was immersed in heavenly sound and then, about twenty minutes into my listening, he paused for a new song.

Three chords and I knew. The song you always asked for from our jazz pianist friends. 'Send in the Clowns.' The song our dear friend, Vinnie Hill, played at your memorial service on the Hudson River in Upper Nyack. A framed picture of you, sitting on a horse, you in a grand black cape and cocked, brimmed, Australian outback hat, with your grand smile, gracing the big grand piano.

'Send in the Clowns.' Dear one, my heart stopped. The beauty of it all and you almost overwhelmed me. I wept silently, in my soft chair, as he played verse after verse without words. But I remembered. "Isn't it rich?" "Are we a pair?" "Send in the clowns."

Carl, our life was like that. So rich, so much a pair, such fun.

Tonight, talking with you, I feel the richness of the moment and richness of the memories. Such good fortune, I have. How blessed we both are.

CHAPTER 7

REMEMBERING

It is mid-May and we all are flying to Madison, Wisconsin. Teri, David, Asher and Erickson are coming from North Carolina and Randy, Bonnie, Lauren, Tammy, Dave and me from San Francisco. Teri and Tammy are bulging in their pregnancies, all of us are trying to have a good time. Swimming in the motel pool, being on the UW campus, where you and I met and studied and played.

Saturday, May 17, what would have been our 39th wedding anniversary, we make our way to the University Arboretum. We think about your before sunup trips with our three young kids to see the rising sun prairie beauty here and the many times we came to the arboretum for picnics. Remember, Carl?

The lilacs are in bloom now, at their peak. The same purple clusters and sweet perfume filled the altar of my little Baptist church in Whitehall on that special day – today our wedding day.

We are remembering you, gathered in a circle, barely talking but for some choked words of fondness, sweetness, love. We bid you a fond farewell to earthly form as we quietly walk through the lilacs and scatter your ashes to the earth, to the soft warm air.

Deep in our own thoughts, we go to the UW campus and the Wisconsin Union. Downstairs in the Rathskeller, our friends and relatives are waiting to greet us and hug us. It is good to be with people you and we know in a place you and I loved. We all remember you, our own memories blending with the next. You are certainly loved.

On June 16, 1997, Isaac Carl Radmer Smith is born to Teri and David. What a tribute to you – your name imprinted in all of Isaac's lifetime and your genes imprinted on a quarter of his. I kissed the small, framed photo of you with your last love note to me on the wall of my apartment and told you of his birth.

New life, Carl! It is awesome. New life to replace the old! Please, don't take offense! We all die someday, as you know better than I do, if you are really truly in that other world where the souls pass on, that I'm so close to believing. You just died too soon, before we were ready. But, perhaps that's always the case. You never want to let go of your nearest and dearest and you might even feel bad about someone you don't particularly care for who died. Because death makes us confront our own mortality. That's part of the sadness. We are reminded with your or anyone's death that life does not go on forever for me or anyone. We take death personally. I am going to die, too. I just don't know when.

I know someone who believes that Methuselah, as said in the Old Testament in the Bible, did in real life live a full 969 years and that others in that time lived almost that long. Can you imagine that? Well, I guess you dear Carl would see even 969 as a blip on the screen of eternity and infinity. I wonder if 969 years would be long enough for someone with an insatiable appetite for years – like me. But if you believe it, the spirit does live on forever. I'm not sure what I believe though I do feel your spirit. It's a conundrum for me. I feel you so strongly, I hear your words and talk with you, yet question if a part of you, a ghost of you, still exists. The bets for me lean toward your spirit living on.

August 5th and it has been six months since you died. I walked on Ocean Beach and remembered. I talked with Randy. He has a candle still burning from yesterday for you. We all lit candles. I cried on the phone with Teri. Bonnie invited me over for dinner, knowing it was probably a difficult time for me. I shed a few tears before I left them and buckets more at home during the night. A wellspring of sadness I feel with the missing and the memories. And you came through, dear Carl. I heard you clearly in my head saying, "I love you."

Carl, you have life force! You are present in our hearts and in new life. Two months after Isaac came into this world Tammy gave birth to a girl, Melia. Your genes are passed on again. No question, part of you lives on.

CHAPTER 8
PEOPLE

Carl, we know with the new births of Isaac and Melia, that part of your legacy is children and our children's children. It might not have happened. Maybe we wouldn't have been able to have kids, though we wanted them. Maybe our three wouldn't have married nor had children. We didn't have expectations and were just joyous in the moment with each other. People are perfectly content without progeny. Children are not a requirement for happiness and, for some, can even be a deterrent to a happy state. But for us they came and we loved it. We have invested a lot of time in their lives. It has been a rich part of our being. And now, dear Carl, with you gone, they continue to enrich my life.

We keep cooking up things. Tammy and I met at Stacey's Book Store downtown to see and hear Dr. Andrew Weil talk. 'Don't look to others for healing," he said. "You heal yourself.' How appropriate is that! In the spring Tammy and Dave and I saw the Japantown cherry blossoms and ate at a vegan restaurant, Now and Zen. We three have seen 'Sling Blade' at the artsy Lumiere Theater on California and Van Ness. They planned with other good friends, a Mothers' Day picnic in wine country. Tammy had us over for a Hawaiian slide show and supper.

Randy and Bonnie and Lauren have had cookouts, treating me

with dinners out, and parties for special days. They've driven us to Sausalito and the army barracks and museum on the water and we've had good visits on my sofa. I have little Lauren over a lot and all the family come, now and then, for a usually take out meal

I don't do much cooking. You took over in your early retirement years, vegetarian cooking, no less. Now, I buy simple food, wash vegetables and fruits and eat them raw. I drink wheat grass juice at Jamba Juice just down my hill. My life is becoming more and more stripped of ornament.

Teri and her family flew from North Carolina to San Francisco in the summer and stayed with me. We fell in love with your namesake, infant Isaac Carl Radmer Smith. And while they were here, Melia, our grandchild number five arrived! I wish you were here to meet them. All our family filled our days with the Monterey Aquarium, Alcatraz, the Randall Museum, and to Chevy's and the Blue Front Café in the Haight for eating. What fun we all had together!

Friends and relatives frequent this city and I have lots of room for guests. We eat at the Beach Chalet and watch the waves wash over Ocean Beach where I walk frequently. I drive us to Marin and more beaches or to Palo Alto for a macrobiotic dinner gathering with people I know. We take the MUNI downtown and climb steep California Avenue to Grant Street for a free noon classical concert at the Old Saint Mary's Cathedral. Though, I live alone, people are a big part of the day.

And then there are the new. I meet people every day. Some

more than once and a few have even become friends. In line at the Post Office, reading at the Mechanic's Library, having discussions at the Commonwealth Club, the talks and walks. It's a friendly place here and I'm an outgoing person, as you know.

I could call all the people in my life a distraction from the grief. But to be distracted is not the driving impulse for me. My impulse is to confront the grief and be rid of it, not to hide it or be afraid of it. I do what I do because I want to do it. I do like to be with people and that adventurous spirit leads me on for action.

But people are not perfect and relationships with friends or family are not perfect either. There can be family slights and hurts. I've had my share and I don't always know what to do about it. They don't want to talk about it so I let the hurts hang around until they recede with all my activity and love of life. Or I feel the hurts until they dissipate with my internal dialogue exploring beliefs. That is, I, big I, take the responsibility to get rid of my hurt even though I might feel someone else is at fault. With internal work I can feel good without discussing it with them, since they don't want discussion. They are pretty powerful people if they can make me feel bad. I have built up a lot of internal strength through the years to handle what comes my way and to be ok with it. I work to change myself, not other people.

What about forgiveness? Does that help? If someone has slighted me, doesn't see the error in their ways (that's my perception and judgment), doesn't apologize and perhaps never will, what am I left to do? Cry in my soup? Carry a grudge for the rest of my life? Keep feeling bad about it? I can let it go –easy to say – or I can go through a process of forgiveness. I listened to a cassette tape on forgiveness early on in my grief and I cried my heart out over my hurts. I talked out loud in my tears and forgave people who I thought had hurt me. It was a useful exercise and I let go of at least some of the pain. But it goes deeper than that. I am judging my daughter, for example, if I think that she is remiss in not being there for me. Here is a more global view. You don't have to forgive if you don't judge in the first place.

Friends from the past can appear and disappear quickly. People are very caught up in their own lives and don't always extend themselves like I might wish they would. New people, potential friends, can let you down. Plans that I took seriously, they might not even remember. Even though I'm good at it, it's work to make friends. You meet people, like them, get together again, put time and energy into it and one or the other loses interest. So many possible friends fall by the wayside and so many do not make the effort I do. I get exhausted with it.

Carl, I have talked with you in spirit about this and I said that I feel sometimes that I don't have any lasting friends. You wondered sometimes too, if you had any lasting friends and after your death everyone is saying wonderful things about you. Your advice to me was, "Be content to be alone. Be patient. Keep looking."

What I have found is that I feel abrasions to my tired psyche more intensely now, than I did in the past. I feel bruised, not as strong.

And I know why. I am in a more vulnerable state. My psyche has been exposed, laid bare with losing you. It's as if a shield, a protective cushion has been lost to reveal my fragile state. You helped ease the sting of perceived hurts. You were that cushion for the bumps and lumps on the road.

Knowing that gives me some perspective, but a hurt is a hurt at the time and I don't want to anesthetize the pain. You know me, no drugs! I don't want to cover up the discomfort.

Carl, many nights in bed I have talked with your spirit about the 'discomforts of the psyche.' I've wondered where my newly found balance was. I have felt awfully shaky on those nights, a 'gyro night' as my friend Barbara calls it. But I know that I'm trying my best. So I feel good about that! And Carl, your attentive spirit is right with me, you hear me and understand. People say, "Be good to yourself" and I hear you saying it too.

What I would wish for is a solution – literal and figurative – to magically dissolve the plaques of resistant angst. They clog up the thinking and the joy. I imagine that a potion would be good for our kids, too, with their own private angst and pain and hurts.

We have no magic potion. So, we blunder and flounder through our days and at the same time celebrate our lives, making the most of our existence, of having each other and being together.

People are a part of my day or week, but I'm a loner, too. As you know, I want my own time. I love the quiet and solitude of just me.

Thank goodness, or I might have a really, really tough time without you.

The risk of having those alone times, though, is that my exposed self is more apparent to me. The pain is not muted with action. I feel my bare soul. I face it, though, and see a kind of beauty in who I am. Tears and cheers, human to the core. And magnificent. A gift of the gods, I am. You, dear one, are a gift in another form. Thank you, Carl and the Universe.

CHAPTER 9
SEARCHING

You and I have always been searchers of truth and clarity in the midst of firm opinions and muddled thinking. We are hunters of answers to the big questions in life – what started it all, why are we here and what happens to us when we die. We have not had the comfort of religious beliefs to answer those big questions.

Well, now that you are gone, what do I find myself doing? Keeping up the search! I'm going to talks and discussions on death. I'm sampling Eastern religions. I'm hearing and meeting big name psychics in big hotel conference rooms. The attraction to exploring those questions about the mysteries of life is big time for me and I am finding that the programs are out there big time in the Bay area, my home. It's as if some person or maybe the intelligence guiding the planets planned this for me. Or is it your precious spirit leading the way? I can hardly miss the happenings. California is prime territory for such searching. Here's a sample, spirit Carl.

Dannion Brinkley, author of 'Saved By the Light,' for starters. Or endings – ha! His life ended at least three times. I believe him. And he came back to life. After his talk to hundreds, he hugged me twice in the line of people talking to him. I'm not sure how it happened, but I can use hugs! Rosemary Allen of 'Life After Death.' John Edward of book and TV fame. I left his large crowd early, I became so impatient with his channeling – too many reality checks with survivors and too simple messages from the deceased. That doesn't mean, though, that I don't believe in the afterlife.

Deepak Chopra was at the Palace of Fine Arts. You and I used to listen to his tapes in the car. We both liked his creative and intelligent thinking on the mind and body. There are a lot of mysterious forces at work that we don't know about or understand and I want to explore it. Deepak is mesmerizing in person.

I've heard lectures on every 'other worldly' subject. 'Mars and the Origin of Life – Search For Alien Life,' 'Other Planets' and 'The Ape and Evolution' at the Commonwealth Club. 'Beyond Grief, Surviving Loss' at UCSF.

I've joined the Epicureans to discuss philosophy and ask the big questions at the Dolores Café or at Kirby Cove on Stinson Beach. I love this group and join in eagerly. I go to my friend, Dr. Hal Sarf's weekly seminars arguing the views of Hegel, Neitzsche, Descartes, and of course Plato and Socrates. Call me of the Socratic school, whose noble sentiment was "Know thyself." Existence as a whole spurs me to seek insight into myself. Carl if you do exist in a different form and on another plane from mine, that fact makes existence more complete for me to learn about myself. Plato would say that possessing wisdom transforms the self and guides it through life's pain and uncertainty. Because of your death Carl, I am gaining knowledge about myself that

I might not have known.

I spent a day at Spirit Rock Meditation Center in Marin, with my friend, Ann, to be in the presence of the live goddess, Devi, following in a Hindi as well as Buddhist tradition. Large baskets of fresh fruit offerings were on the altar and I was tempted to take something (I love fresh fruit), but I did not succumb to the urge. The Buddhist followers seemed almost too reverential, to my discomfort. Respect is one thing. Deifying is another. I don't have it in me to deify.

I've been in meditation at a Hindu Temple, somewhat soothing, but for me, hollow in meaning. I've been to the Zen Buddhist Center in the Haight, good for meditation. When Robert Thurman is in town, he makes an appearance there.

Greengulch Farm, in Marin, suits me better. The gardens of vegetables and flowers are tended to lovingly by the residents and volunteers. Bonnie has volunteered here and enjoys the physical labor and preparing the organic vegetables for meals and for sale. I have hiked through a few times, coming from the ocean and nearby trails. Salty moist air wafts over from Muir Beach, which is almost within view. The Zen Buddhist practitioners gather in the zendo and meditate. Some useful platitudes come from a speaker. I like the ambiance. No one seems better than anyone else. But I haven't taken on any new beliefs and I have made only two trips back to the meeting rooms.

Remember, Carl, when I took a course with the Dalai Lama at MIT in Boston for a day? As the spiritual and temporal leader of the

Tibetan people and as a man committed to his strict Buddhist practices, I have had such admiration for him. You dropped me off on the campus and I sat right under his nose in the front row. I learned that Tibetan monks are able to sit in lotus position in freezing weather and evaporate wet sheets draped over their backs. This is the height of, as my dad would have said, 'mind over matter.' I wish our 'mind over matter' approaches had worked with your cancer. But some force had another intention. I can almost accept that, I think, but it's dealing with the aftermath of death, my grief, that is tough. I am missing you and longing for your presence.

Well, Carl, I have spent another day with His Holiness the Dalai Lama. He spoke at the Civic Auditorium, across from City Hall, in my city. Security was very tight. Years ago in Boston, we had no checking of our personage or possessions at all. The world changes, not always in ways we like. This time I sat in the back row of a crowd of thousands. Reincarnation, which my Dad believed in and wrote about, though he was an agnostic (he picked and chose his own beliefs!), is a central tenet in Tibetan Buddhist thinking. I still can't quite accept it, though it makes a lot of practical sense, the recycling of souls. My skeptical mind yearns for more evidence.

Here is another 'remember,' Carl. You and I visited the Edgar Cayce Center in Virginia Beach. On tests, we both scored high in ESP. I want that to manifest now! Show me you are out there! I'm working on it and am trying to reach you with those special powers.

Ann, an astrologer friend, whom you and I both met in Nepal, came over to my place in San Francisco and did hours and pages of readings on you (your physical body not needed) and me. You and I are remarkably in sync and she was on the mark for describing you. She confirmed for me the ways things were and are. I can't say that I learned anything except that you have purpose in passing on to your new world. I think the message from the stars and planets was for you to regroup with the souls and bask in nirvana, the supernal, after your hard-earned lessons on earth.

Do I have purpose? Yes! It comes from inside me, not from an outside dictate. I intend to be the best person I can be. I am learning so much through this grief, about myself, about others, about giving and being grateful. I was happy with myself before you died, but I do think Carl, that I am an even better person now than I was. Come back and we'll be dynamite together!

In October, I lived at the Option Institute in Massachusetts for four weeks. Exploring happiness, a non-judging attitude, acceptance, love and beliefs. The founders Bears' and Samaria's philosophy is that happiness is a choice. Other people don't make us sad. We are sad or anxious or hurt because of the beliefs that we have. In a dialogue with a mentor we find and examine our beliefs and change them if we choose. I learned about the healing power of unconditional love. Mmmmmm. What a feast that was. I came back to San Francisco, full to the brim with new insights and good feelings.

It has been almost a year since you left us. I would not have wished it or asked for it. An adventure to put it mildly, more squarely, an upheaval of big proportion. We're all still recovering and learning and taking deep breaths and looking to the stars. Carl, are you up there?

CHAPTER 10
ANNIVERSARY

Tomorrow, January 5, 1998, Sunday, 11:45am, North Carolina (your spirit ascension site) time, 8:45am, San Francisco time, it will be one year since you died. This morning, Saturday, I read from 'Living Through Personal Crisis' by Ann Stearns. So many things hit me right. What strikes me is that we're dealing with death, but I am ALIVE. I lived through this. You passed on.

Some nice phone calls came and then I walked to Golden Gate Park and, by chance, came on a psychic fair. Are things by chance or by grand design? A Kirlian photographer took my photo, revealing a purple and magenta aura around my upper body. "It's magic," he said. "You're making a big step to release things of the past." Well, I'm doing my best, I thought.

The day has been full of reflection. In the evening I felt moved to honor you formally with a candle, exactly 12 hours before the anniversary of your death. Standing at the sink, I poured my heart out to you. I talked with you and cried. "Carl, I love you so much and wish you were here. I want you so much." You said, "You have done great! I'm proud of you. Be happy. Have fun." "Hug me," I said "and then I will let you go." I pleaded, "Carl, show me some sign! Please, give me a signal, a sound, a touch, a sight. I want you!" Then I turned my head around and amazingly, the alarm on your wristwatch started ringing! Exactly at 8:45pm.

Now, I've been wearing that watch, with links taken out to fit me, ever since you died. I only turn the dials to change the time in my travels. I have not even attempted to use or affect any of the other features of your weathered silver timepiece. I racked my brain. Have I heard the buzz go off before? I don't remember any buzzing the past year but I am remembering that it may have gone off several times in the past week, at random times. I reflexively pushed a post to stop the ringing and hardly gave it a thought. I have not ever set the alarm. And this time, after several beeps, the ringing stopped on its own. Carl, I am left to think, it is you. Only tonight did I imagine this as a signal from you, something you would set up and accomplish in a spirit state to reach out to me. You were the electrical engineer genius who could do anything with electronics. It's your medium. It would be a natural for you to pick your watch as the instrument to show me a sign. This past week the random rings may have been 'preview alerts.' What a perfect way to reach me, if you were having trouble getting your words across. I hear, "Listen! I'm here! I knew this would get your attention. I'm alive and well. Wake up to your new life!" Oh, the wonderment of it all!

Carl, you were with me. I felt your arms around me, though I did not feel the physical pressure of a touch. You said, "I love you." I am choosing to believe that your spirit was with me and was embracing me. Just allow me a thread of the skeptic or a hint of straddling, After all, unlike you, I am still of the earth, with at least one foot on the ground.

It's Sunday morning and almost 8:45am. I am not expecting any high drama today. I just want a soothing yoga session with you in mind. I move your candle from the counter to the floor, along with a clock and a photo that our Pulitzer Prize winning friend, Nat Fine took of you. So vital you look, standing in our house on the hill in New York, with your ever-present smile. I start out with 'Homage to the Sun,' stretched out and folded up. In the 'Tree,' we stand so tall and straight and balanced. 'Lotus' you did wherever we were. Your vitality is catching. I feel life surging in all my positions.

I talk to you and you talk back. "It has been a difficult year. I've made adjustments and I did the best I could. I loved you to the end." "It has been a good life with you. I love you."

In your honor, I turned on your computer. I've had a fear of doing it. And I've had my own computer to use. The first thing that came on the screen was the date and the time, you set it up to do. I felt a little jolt. January 5, 1998. Right on. The computer hasn't missed a beat. Something of yours was pulsing the past year, besides your watch. I feel like I am taking up where I left off with you.

It's cold in San Francisco, today. I took a walk down my hill and up the long hill to UCSF to warm up and I take in the view of downtown from the library lounge. The crown of Saint Ignatius Church stands out on the campus of the University of San Francisco. The hilly rolling landscape is filled with rooftops and fronts of Victorians in soft colors. Looking back to the book stacks, I see on the first rack, the "New England Journal of Medicine." That was one of several references that informed Randy what a lethal disease you had. He gave up hope then and he was right. I head back out into the chill air and return home.

At five o'clock, Randy and Bonnie and Lauren pick me up and we meet Tammy's family at Greens, a vegetarian restaurant on the water. The Marina is filled with boats. One of your last dreams for us was to live in a boat and sail and motor to unfound places. Too soon, you left your earthly moorings and found another place.

Over dinner, with our family, I tell my story of my talking to you at the sink and then your watch alarm going off. "That's' cool," Dave said. The others sat in quiet fascination.

For you, I wore gold – a bracelet, top and printed skirt – to show how enriched we are with your life. Trying to talk about you is difficult for everyone, with tears riding the surface. I said something about my gratefulness for you and how accepting you were of all of us. You didn't try to change us. You were a wonderful person. Dave felt it an honor to have known you. I acknowledged that it has been a difficult year, but that we all have done the best we could. Tammy agreed and all with grateful understanding nodded their heads.

Our tender hearts felt safe in the embrace of family. It was good to all be together with you. Thank you, dear Carl, for the memories.

CHAPTER 11

ONWARD

There are things I want to do. I have a life ahead of me, as well as the present moment to relish. Singing, for one, and whatever else comes up on my spacious pallet of possibilities. Now that the one-year mark has passed, I somehow feel a little freer and ready to move on. You have told me many times from your spirit world to be happy and enjoy life and I've tried and partially succeeded. But I want more pleasure out of life and less angst.

On day one of my new year, I meet a new male friend, as we had planned, for coffee and we talk about a myriad of things, but especially about taking walks and climbs. In the evening I climb that long hill to UCSF and audition for a choral group. Yes, audition! How brave I am singing new music alone and with several others, unaccompanied, with tricky timing and note changes, on the stage in Cole Hall. I've sung alone and in groups before, but it has been a long time, and I'm feeling my sea legs. My voice is a little shaky. But Carl, I passed!

What joy it is to be part of this group, The San Francisco Choral Society. The music is majestic, ageless and brilliant.

Brahm's "German Requiem." Haydn's "Lord Nelson Mass in D Minor." Mozart's "Mass in C." Rachmaninoff's "Vespers" and Britten's' "Rejoice in The Lamb." Marek Jasinski's "Alleluja" and Morton

Lauridsen's "Ubi Caritas Et Amor." It thrills me to even say the names of these composers and works. We sing A cappella works by Pablo Casals' "O Vos Omnes," Johannes Brahms' "Darthulas Grabesgesang" and Moses Hogan's "Ev'ry Time I Feel The Spirit." Over time we do homage to those composers and many others in Davies Symphony Hall, Saint Ignatius Church and other churches and even under the dome of City Hall. And my family comes to bask in the beauty. I wink surreptitiously to them in the balcony.

I love the music. It is so reflective of all of my senses, my ruminations and my appreciation. I feel grief, sadness and yearning, and reverence, love and glory in the singing. It radiates to me and through me and from me.

Brahms himself said, "Now I am consoled…I feel like an eagle, soaring ever higher and higher." Oh Brahms, I am so in tune with you! I feel so consoled with the beauty of the music. I am floating to new heights, perhaps to where your spirits dwell. Carl, you're in good company!

It is Sunday and Tammy called to invite me to go with the three of them to the tidal pools at Moss Beach. Dave drives us south as far as the Half Moon Bay Airport, where we turn toward the ocean and park. With Melia being carried in a baby backpack on Dave's shoulders, we head into the cold, penetrating wind off the water. Just south of us is Mavericks off Pillar Point, where surfers from around the world compete. They come with a day's notice if the waves are high, in the winter. But it is late January, just north of the point and we are alone. We are wedged between the water and the eroding cliff, so typical of California beaches. The tide is out to reveal the tidal pools, uncommon treasures on the coastline. A ways out, the waves are crashing over large rocks exposed in low tide, making a rhythmic, thunderous sound. There are a few brown seals, hanging out on the rocks, warming in the sun.

We walk in the sand where the shallow pools are, cautiously skittering over the rough rocks that are very slippery with green, almost moss-like seaweed. Our feet and our hands are numbed as we test the very cold clear waters. How in the moment we are! The sandy floors of the scattered but contiguous pools are covered with crushed, glittering shells, iridescent colors sparkling in the sun. Orange and green starfish, tentacles reaching, are well secured to the rocks. Beautiful sea anemones, turquoise and purple and burgundy, are floating just below the surface of the water, attached underneath to the reef.

There is even more life! Dipping down, we see small fish darting around and little crabs scurrying about. A conflux of mussels, blue and black, are clustered around each other. Strands of flat, fibrous, shiny kelp float aimlessly. We look, we feel, we breathe in the cold air and feel warmed by the sun. Time stands still. I don't know if minutes or hours have gone by.

Life, in all its glory. Nature with its mystery. Beauty, not of our doing. We are in rapture. Slowly, we walk to the car. Tammy, Dave, Melia and I have been intimate today with a fascinating, intricate seascape and natural beauty, so real, but almost beyond belief. I'll feast for time to come.

How fortunate I am, Carl. Prodigious gifts are in my life. I treasure my family. I can take in beauty with all my senses. I have talent from some power beyond myself to create in exciting and gratifying ways. Life is good, even without you, my dearest, no longer nearest, except when I feel your spirit, which I do now. "I am glad for you, Ethel. Be brave. You are doing just what I knew you would do. Exploring and getting the most you could out of life. I embrace you, my love."

It's Valentine's Day. I feel tugs for you, Carl, in my heart and thoughts. The memories are strong. We were lovers and I miss you greatly. My urge, though, is not to bemoan, but to be active and take my almost daily walk on Ocean Beach. I walk twice today, once with a friend and once alone. When walking alone, I was thinking about my pink quartz heart, that my massage therapist suggested I buy. I decided, while walking, that I would have a hole drilled in the top (ouch!), a fixing put in and a chain and wear it as a pendant, close to my heart. Pink quartz conveys calm and tranquility and loving myself, sentiments I feel and want. Just then, something written in the sand caught my eye and I walked back to look. A large heart was drawn, with these words inside, "I Love Me." Wow! Did someone read my thoughts? I have instant confirmation! Yes! I DO love myself. Sometimes, I am hard on myself, replaying tapes of hurtful times. There is no use in that. It's good to be reminded to be kind to my sometimes, fragile self, to be

CONVERSATIONS WITH CARL: My Journey Through Grief

easy and be good to me. I look at my red turtleneck that I have on to commemorate the day and I take in the heartfelt message.

Randy and Bonnie and dear little Lauren had me over to their house just around the corner of the block from my apartment at the end of the day. We exchanged hugs and kisses and valentines. Lauren had drawn a red heart on white paper with a two and a half years old child's script, "I love you, Grandma Ethel!" It has been a veritable love fest today!

Kate Michelman, President of NARAL, National Abortion Rights Action League, talked at the Commonwealth Club and I attended. Now, I am not for abortion by any stretch, but I do want to keep it out of the back allies and let doctors perform it legally, when needed, without their hands being tied. I worked hard and was a leader for this cause, in the '70s and '80s. I spoke with Kate about working in the trenches. She's a lovely person and she wondered why I came to San Francisco. When I said my husband died, her sweetness and understanding showed, "I am so sorry.," she offered. And then, on learning of my present life, she said, "Congratulations on making a new life for yourself!" Thank you, Kate. I feel so good with that. I did create a whole new life and it's a good one.

And that reminds me, Carl. I am tired of causes. I did my bit for so many worthy groups, through the years. Let others take over. Now, I take pleasure in squeezing the most out of and into my new life. Curiosity is a driving force. I want to learn everything about everything and do whatever I can and want to do and haven't done.

The lectures at UC Medical are regular fare for my appetite. I just heard a talk on naturopathy, which I do know a lot about. What interested me was the story of the speaker's husband, a medical doctor, who had lymphoma. They went wherever they could find alternative healing and also did chemotherapy and a bone marrow transplant. It was a positive experience for them. What we did, Carl, was a positive experience for us too. The doctor with lymphoma died after 10 years. You, dear husband, died four months after you were diagnosed with cancer. I wanted a day more, a week more, a month more, or a year. Is our time on this earth never enough?

AARP thinks you are still here, as do numerous money management groups and financial institutions, no matter what I tell them. I have tried and tried to cancel your AARP membership (you knew I didn't like associating with the word 'old' or with the single-minded politics of the group, which was 'we're entitled to all the benefits we can get' kind of thinking), and the bulletins and promotions keep coming. They and others have even tracked down your new abode, which is mine, though you never lived in San Francisco. I announce to all, "Your new address is the stars!"

I occasionally feel my parental roots, which are Swedish. Remember our two visits to Sweden, Carl, one time with our pre-teen children? We were immersed in family. Such kindness and hospitality emanated from them and I used my very halting Swedish to talk with my mother's cousin and my aunt, Elizabet. Here in San Francisco, to get a flavor of the Scandinavian, I took MUNI Bus 43 to the water and attended a monthly Swedish Sunday service at the Norwegian Seaman's Church. I felt like I was in Sweden! My voice was full and strong as I sang longingly, hymns in Swedish: "Tryggare Kan Ingen Vara" (Children of the Heavenly Father), "Dag For Dag Ogenblick I Sander" (Day By Day and With Each Passing Moment), and "Jag Har En Vin Som Alskar Mig" (I Have A Friend Who Loveth Me). I admired the table spread of kringlor, sma kaka, brod and smor and syltt and ost. Bowls for berries were filled with jordgubba and lingonmousse, A blond woman served kaffe with socker and gradde. I mixed with people that had a strong resemblance to each other. The view of the Bay from our elegant space in the Marina, partway up the hill, was calm and picture perfect. I took in the serene splendor.

But, even with that savorous experience I confess to feeling lonely. It comes on me sometimes. I remember the fun of the past with you and I want you here in the present. It's hard to get over 39 years of togetherness, Carl. You see my sad heart, I know you do. I almost know what you are going to say. "Ethel, we're reading each other's thoughts. I see your tears. Let them come. It's good to open up and let the sadness out. My love for you is greater than ever. Feel a kiss. I'm with you."

Oh Carl that's more than I even hoped for. It means so much to me. That is you. Please, hang around for awhile. I need that especially now, in my melancholic state of mind. I just knew you would answer.

Thanks and love from me.

I'm feeling my roots again, this time in Wisconsin, our birth state, where we earned our degrees, married and raised our children to school age. A couple of years before you died we looked for lake property on the Eagle River Chain of Lakes in the Wisconsin Northwoods. We had sold our East Coast properties and were free of ownership ties. Years ago in the Adirondack Mountains of New York, we had built a unique smart-looking boat house and a bedroom and screen porch addition to a lake cabin. Creating, designing and building was our thing and we were good at it. Tempted with new Wisconsin terrain, we had such fun designing yet more lake homes, but we never bought any land.

Well, I'm dreaming again for both of us. My sister found land for sale and I flew out and looked at it. Within a day I signed the papers and it's mine. There are luxurious tall pine filling the sloping lot to the waters of Hiawatha, facing the setting sun and an orange glow rippling across the lake's reflective surface. It is my flight of fancy. Maybe someday I'll build a place and maybe I won't. But it's all my own. I want to dream.

I'm doing good things for myself and treating myself well. Such nice experiences I'm having in this new life. I imagine you Carl being with me on almost all these occasions and really do feel your spirit. It is so real, so natural and comfortable, You are a cozy presence. And Carl, I am realizing happiness without you. I know you want that for me. My artist's palette is filling with living colors and there is room for more.

CHAPTER 12

MOVEMENT

Movement is synonymous with life. To be alive is to move. If there is the slightest stirring in a one-celled creature, it is alive. On a grander scale, my human body is an animate being. A self-impelled twitch evinces life. More complex motions of the dance or a climb showcase my existence.

You dear Carl are dead, I say it straight out. Your body is dead and turned to ashes, spread to the winds and the earth. Like Humpty Dumpty, we can't put you back together again. We can't breathe life into you even if we could reclaim your body in demise. We needed movement in your body for life and there was none. Your spirit is another story. It is certainly alive in me and I suspect out there. I've had evidence of your spirit presence. But your earthly form, sad to say, has expired.

Movement is my life. When you died I moved across the continent to a new life. And move I did. On the move. Action packed. Energy filled. On the go, in one form or another, from morning 'til night. Brain power. Mental convolutions and gyrations. Emotional whirls and swirls in a vortex of feelings. And most of all, physical action. Moving my body is vital to all parts of my being, mental and emotional included. When in motion, I seem to heal. The mind calms and the sadness dissipates while I am climbing the hills of San Francisco. My blood flows, my muscles stretch and pull, my joints jump. Endorphins kick in.

The hills are right outside my window and door. The capacious Golden Gate Park is three blocks down my hill. It is a quick ride to other parks and the beaches edging the western side of the city. Just north across the Bay, are the rolling headlands and beaches of Marin. Down the coast are more beaches and mountains, a geological wonder. On arrival in this playground for people in motion, I didn't skip a beat.

I walked and walked. Up and down the hills, around the blocks, to the park and through the park, around Lake Merced, to shops and restaurants, to my children's houses. And to Grand View Park, just up my hill and a long stair climb, to see the grandest of views in a panorama as I circle the top of this windy promontory.

Taking in the field of view from south to west to north to east is breathtaking. And I'm catching my breath from the hefty climb. The air feels good. My lungs are expanding, I can tell. My heart beats with confidence, pumping that red vital fluid to my muscles, which are making a claim for more oxygen. I feel almost euphoric with the ascent. There is no room for sadness here. I feel whole. I am alive!

It takes just a walk in the park with my grandchildren, usually one at a time, to raise my spirits if they are low. Lauren and I have tea and salty brown glazed crackers shaped like a crescent moon, in the Japanese Teahouse after roaming the Tea Garden, spending time with the koi fish and climbing over the arched bridge.

I push Melia in her leopard print upholstered stroller around

Stow Lake. We talk to the ducks and they quack back Her long, dark curled eyelashes flutter and she looks intently at the rippling water. We linger reverently in the red and gold Chinese Pavilion. It feels like a pagoda to me, so we quietly honor all our worldly ancestors. We say 'hi' to the Strybing Arboretum, where we have spent hours wandering on other days, as we pass it on our way home. How sweet and tender the world looks through my little girls' eyes.

Several times a week, I take a ride downtown. Once on Market Street, my legs take over and I walk and climb for hours. It is purposeful. There are events to attend, shops to visit and people to meet, business matters to take care of and book stores and libraries to hang out in.

I also walk with no intention but to stimulate my senses. Up the Embarcadero I go, from the Ferry Building at the end of Market, along the water and through North Beach, where the artsy bohemians used to dwell when I lived in the city as a college graduate intern decades ago. I pass Telegraph Hill and make it to the North Waterfront. Briskly I return to the heart of San Francisco and to my ride home. My own heart is here now, in good shape and very much at home.

When inspired, I've bridged the Bay on foot, crossing the Golden Gate Bridge all the way to Sausalito. I've walked lengths of the map along Judah, forty blocks to the Pacific Ocean in one stretch. I've joined 80,000 runners, partway into the run and with a mix of running and walking, for the 'Bay to Breakers Race,' a span on the map from water to water. Dave and Melia cheer me on from the sidelines as I run past them and wave. I feel the high-spirited energy of the group and it doesn't matter that I run alone.

The breakers draw me most. Ocean Beach as well as Thornton Beach further south, below Fort Funston where the hang gliders fly, has hundreds of miles of my imprints in the sand.

High tide is the most exciting. Some stretches of the beach are narrower because of the cliff wall being closer to the sea. Will I make it from the more expansive beach, through the narrow part between the cliff and the relentless water, to where it spreads out again? Can I scurry over the slippery rocks fast enough to not get totally sloshed or even overcome by the next incoming wave? I don't want to be battered by the rocks or swept out to sea, so I don't take big chances. As I walk, I time the waves and observe the height and strength. Maybe it's a myth, but I find the seventh wave, the Biblical God's favorite number and mine as well, to be appropriately the most powerful, God's majesty showing itself.

So I wait for the biggest arch of water to begin to recede and I take off like a gazelle. Leaping, running, jumping on and over the rocks, it's a race with time. I feel wonderful. I am superwoman! All parts are working well together. I rise to the urgency of the moment. The adrenaline is flowing, with a little dash of fear thrown in. Through the narrow passage I spurt, to the safety of the widening sand.

Is there a metaphor here for me? I'm not sure. Am I a risk taker? Yes. Am I feeling free and strong and here's the chance to show it? I think so. Do I want to get to the other side? I do. It is as simple as the riddle, 'Why did the chicken cross the road? To get to the other side.' Whatever presents itself on my path, I deal with, and continue on my way. Just as I have done, Carl, with your death. I want to get to the other side. Movement helps to get me there. What I want most from my daring though, is to be in motion. All parts are moving in harmony. The body and the mind are awake, alert and alive.

My favorite beach is Pescadero Beach. Its rocky outcropping reaches way out into the ocean. I scramble over and around the sandy rocky terrain, to find a perch and gaze at the sea. I am almost surrounded by the tumbling, foaming water. The waves hitting the large rugged mass of stone are spectacular. I am mesmerized with the sheer power of the waves, as well as the beauty of the ever-shifting cascades of water and foam. There is constant change. Nothing stays the same. In nature or in my life.

Carl, I think of you. I can't help it. My eyes are filling with tears and the watery display around me is blurred. Beauty and heartache resonate so closely in my heartstrings. Speak to me dear heart and pure heart. I want your pure spirit wisdom. My heart has been broken and I'm trying to fix it.

"My dear Ethel, you are so brave. You dare the waves. You see the beauty in the sea. Your body and mind vibrate with life force. Be proud and be glad. Your joy will grow stronger and longer, as you would say in a rhyming way."

I smile. Can this be? It is just like Carl in the flesh to say that. And now, his spirit is right on and he carries on.

My body is ready to move on, though my thoughts linger with the sea. Lost in thought, I make my way back to my car and home.

I met one of my new best friends at a party. Mike is his name. A week later we met for tea and laughs, as he saw me order freshly squeezed wheat grass juice. We watched as the guy pushed bunches of the green grass into a presser and caught the liquid in a shot glass. I drink this potent liquid often, but my friend had never seen anything like it and howled with laughter. I did too! It was really a comic thing to do. But hey, this is California where the nuts and fruits live and maybe I'm one of them!

Laughs tickle the soul and we have had a huge amount of laughs. They vibrate the body, too. I have laughed a lot in my life and find the funny bone in almost anyone. But Mike and I laugh till we ache and then we laugh some more. This happens in the midst of daily happenings and during lengthy, deep, intellectual conversations, which we also have a lot of. We love books, shop for books and talk books with each other. We have movement and action on a lot of fronts.

But, as big as all that is in my new life, we also share a zest for walking, hiking and climbing. My new friend has introduced me to paths, trails, climbs, beaches, mountains and places that I never knew. What a gift this is!

Mike reintroduced me to Pescadero Beach. I had seen it in

passing, years ago, with Carl and Randy and Bonnie, on our way to visit Phipps Ranch. But I hardly remembered it with all the other beaches along the coast to look at or step foot on during that long ago vacation. And now we are on affectionate terms, the beach and I.

Mike does not plan ahead. We are spur of the moment kids with no expectations. But in fact, almost every morning, early, Mike and I call each other to walk on the beach. I've done my yoga and I pick him up in my car and park along Great Highway. We trudge through the heavy sand and pass the dunes, thick with scrubby maritime growth. We notice the level of the tide and usually remember from the day before, if it is coming in or going out. Should we go left or right? It's a toss up, but I usually veer to the right. That can bring us all the way to the Cliff House where the seal rocks start and the sand ends. Then, we could go up and around the curve of road to a point high above the ocean and a most spectacular view. The ocean, the headlands of Marin and the Golden Gate Bridge stand out in a grand sweep. But usually that is a separate hike I make by myself or with visiting friends and family. The expansive scene is especially impressive to fresh eyes.

We walk all the way to the seal rocks with no strong wind in the early morning, just a gentle breeze. A lot of other walkers are out too, some with their pets. The dogs are running so freely in and out of the water and chasing sticks and balls. It is a joy to watch. Their sense of freedom is catching. There is not a care in the world and we are open to the whole universe, out here on the sand.

Mike and I turn around and feel the suns rays rising and are almost blinded by the mirror of light reflecting off the shifting waves. I tip my cap to ward off the rays. All the way back we walk, keeping a steady pace that has warmed me enough to shed my jacket. He teases me about always taking off and putting on the outer layers and I laugh. It's true that I do that. I don't want to be too hot or too cold. But, I think it's healthy to take on and shed freely. I have done it with my move across the country and in simplifying my life. Static is death. Movement is life.

Often, when Mike and I are in the car, ready to go to the beach, he will suggest that we go to Lake Merced or to Marin and to trails and climbs in other places instead of Ocean Beach and we do. I love having a friend, who is spontaneous, like I am. The moment is not preordained. We create it with looseness and fun.

One morning in the early spring, Mike suggested that we cross the bridge and hike in Marin. There are a hundred places we could go and he suggests climbing to the waterfalls. We have had rain and the creek beds are full. Up above there must be a torrent of water coming down. 'Let's do it!' we cry!

So off we go across the Golden Gate, exiting the highway at Sir Francis Drake. In Fairfax, we turn onto Bolinas. I love the names. The road winds through the Mount Tamalpais Game Refuge, past Alpine Lake to Cataract Trail, where I stop the car and we step out onto the path.

We are under a canopy of trees. The luxuriant scents of spruce, hemlock and Douglas fir, in the cool, moist air, fill our lungs. Our ears take in the distant sound of rushing water. The stream is full to the brim, in some places overflowing our path, and we start our rocky ascent. Towering above us is a cluster of coastal redwood trees, the trunks showing their age by hundreds of years of girth. Redwood trees along the coast can reach heights up to 360 feet and some have lived more than 2000 years. They rival Methuselah.

'Sequoia sempervirens,' Latin for redwood tree, means 'ever living.' And in a sense they are ever alive. New redwoods can sprout from a root system, a unique phenomenon for a softwood tree. The genetic material may be passed on from stump to stump.

A forest is a living biological entity, forever changing and renewing itself. There are stages of growth, death, decay and resurrection. And we humans too, are ever changing and renewing.

The water is rushing now and bouncing over a rocky chute on our left as we climb. Around the bend we see the water leaping higher over rock. Higher still the cascades are falling one above the other. Our heads are filled with a deluge of rushing sound. There is no room for anything but natures force. It's a powerful mantra, a vibrating chant. Thoughts are gone. The woebegone does not exist.

Totally awash in the moment, we turn and follow the trail back down. Our heads stay with the waterfalls as we drive home.

Months later, Mike suggests that we do a bigger climb. The

Purisima Redwoods Preserve is on the western slopes of the Santa Cruz Mountains. Mike has hiked it many times in past years. Sometimes athletic friends joined him but they rarely did it more than once. It is a long and strenuous hike and I am eager to go. It is early on a weekday morning and we meet at the trailhead in the canyon. We have the small parking area to ourselves so we should be alone on the trail, at least for a good while. The air is cold and damp and the rays of the early sun are slanting through the dense green growth and tall trunks of the trees.

Ferns, berries and wildflowers greet us as we start up the path. A hardwood forest of tannoak, madrone and Douglas fir, border the canyon, along with coastal scrub. As we climb higher we look down on the Purisima Creek, babbling over rocks, seeming to have a goal in mind, a destination. The creek had to have started gurgling somewhere and now that it is moving along, where does it intend to go? Perhaps it will embark on further ground or reach the journey's end. Movement is its life. Not unlike us hikers springing up at dawn, surging up the trail and at the finish sighing our peroration.

The climb is taking us to sunny places. The sky has opened up and we see vistas of other mountain peaks. Pockets of fog are hanging in the valleys but the sky is clear. I shed my jacket and we have a gulp of water and take in deeply the warming air.

The path aims us mostly up but sometimes down, so that our climb is much higher than straight to the peak. Going up and going down means going up again. But now our trail snakes back and forth and steadily upward. Around the western curve on the northern slope at last we see it. Spread out on the horizon is the Pacific Ocean in all its grandeur.

We are leveling off to a long slight upward grade in a community of trees. It is so cooling under this sunshade that we want to linger, but we keep up the pace. We reach the base of a short path to the top of the mountain and then we start our descent along a width of gravelly ruts, remnants of an historical logging road. Through prairie oak and tall grasses we cheerily bound, our respite after the plodding upward for so long.

After making it to the top, my body feels at its peak. I swing freely and stride nimbly. I call ahead to Mike, "We did so well on that climb! I feel so alive!"

"Yes, it feels good,' he answers. "You did it, Ethel!"

We are a couple of hours into this hike and we have a long way to go. But we move like the breeze, over and around and mostly down. I tilt my head up and see that ahead of us are the redwoods. They are towering, dense and strong. We enter their forest. It is a quiet, majestic world. There is mystery here. An aura of peace surrounds us. This is our meditation. We have found our church in a cathedral of trees.

We are in awe of the longevity of these trees. The trunk girth of some seem huge. They are the elders in this population. Though this is second growth, some redwoods along the coast are so long-lived that it is hard to fathom their life span. We humans by contrast live in an age of impermanence. Our comings and goings are so fleeting. Our lives seem so brief. How ephemeral our mortal world is.

Down, down we go, more thoughtful now. There has been so much to take in and now we reach the bottom of the trail. Bottom to top, straight up, is 1600'. We've probably climbed 2000', winding around and through the mountains of Santa Cruz. My body can rest with the drive home.

Mike and I have done this mountain climb many times. Sometimes it is muddy from rain and the overflowing creek. We meet people on the trail. A botanist friend has shown us edible wild lettuce and other plants of special interest on the trails. We wonder about the mountain lions that populate the acreage of nature preserves. There are stories of sightings, and in other preserves, of attacks on humans. This was their land. We had our own near encounter but didn't meet the lion eye to eye.

On one of our hikes we were coming through the redwood forest with a steep incline on our left and a deep sharp drop on our right. There in front of us was a doe lying on the path, half eaten from the back quarters. Only the front half from its midsection on was left. Its eyes were open. It was a fresh kill. What we surmised was that a mountain lion was consuming it and jumped into the trees with our approach or with someone else's and was waiting to return to its meal. We looked around, knowing it could leap on us in a second if it was there, saw and heard nothing, and continued on our path. Twice on other hikes alone,

Mike had sightings of this beautiful, illusive creature, but I had none.

Action and movement have carried into my annual cross country skiing in the north woods of Wisconsin, lifting weights at a health club and stair climbs throughout San Francisco. I'm not an athlete but just moving in some fashion has helped my psyche be in a more peaceful state and my body to stay in good health. I am soothed in my loss. An appreciation for my life and all life is filling my being.

Carl, you see it and feel it and know it. You want this for me. And I can hear you saying, "You're doing good things for yourself. Good for you."

CHAPTER 13
DANCE

It is a Friday in late January, just over a year since you died. I've had a walk on the beach with my new friend Mike and we come afterward to my place to figure out something on my computer. Later, Randy calls and he and I make plans for him to install some software. He and Teri have talked on the phone and shared computer expertise. With my son's help I will have more computer tools, more capability and more flexibility. Those also sound like nice features for humans to have.

Carl, you were right. In our written conversation back at the Hermitage, I was concerned about my dependency on you for computer help. You said that I would be able to figure out what to do. And if I can't I can ask someone. Well, I didn't even ask. I have had offers and I am so grateful to my friends and family.

In the evening I take the N Judah train to Van Ness Avenue and walk several blocks up to A Clean Well Lighted Place For Books. Gabrielle Roth is in town, from New York City, speaking about her new book, 'Sweat Your Prayers.' She writes about, talks and teaches movement through dance. I hardly need to know more than the title of her book to recognize that our thinking is in harmony.

Dance is movement and action. Movement is a spiritual practice.

Let your emotions come out in the dance. Create your dance in the moment. Dance your prayers.

At the end of her talk she guided us in movement. I stood up from the floor. Others stood by their chairs or stayed sitting. We moved our arms in a flowing way and our fingers and wrists and shoulders followed. We shifted our hips and legs and let the feet and toes join in. I let go of all my body parts and they flowed, jerked and glided. I released my body in a rhythmic way. She spoke of her Moving Center in Mill Valley and I knew I wanted to attend.

What she said about movement meshed with my own beliefs. I could tell that this dance would make bigger for me the benefits of all my movement. It would enhance and add to my action filled life on the hills, mountains and the beaches.

So I took it from there. I danced my own dance and created my own thoughts about the dance. And I eventually made it to the Community Center on Tennessee Valley Road and joined her tribe of dancers.

Kathy, Jonathan, Gary, and for special workshops, Gabrielle were all leaders of the tribe. With Kathy as our leader on a Thursday morning in February, I danced from 10:15 to noon.

Movement meditation is the phrase for the dance. It is done to very, very loud music, at least to my non-teenage ears. I asked for the volume of the electronic music to be turned down and it was a little, but slowly it crept back up. By that time though, I had immersed myself in the sound. Synthesizers, the tabla and twanga, drums of Kabuki and Taos and Conga, vocal sounds, blocks and shakers, claps and bells, guitars and flutes filled my senses. Pulsing rhythm and a jerking beat vibrated my body.

The map for the dance comes in five rhythms, as directed by Gabrielle. Time is given to each one in our dance and in a prescribed order.

Flowing comes first. Our bodies are warmed up with movements flowing into each other. Staccato is next with snap and jump in our bones. That leads to Chaos, which lets us into the abyss. The fourth rhythm is Lyrical with fluidity, the aftermath of the Chaos of letting go. We move into Stillness, subtle and quiet. Slowly wc come to rest, feeling the movement of our breath and beat of our hearts.

This is what I did with the five rhythms. Flowing with the music seemed instinctive. My fingers slipped through the air, followed by my wrists, elbows and shoulders. My hips slid up and my knees extended themselves, my ankles and toes stretched out to glide around the room. Dozens of others were moving in their own way. We slid and slipped past and around each other, somehow not colliding but often touching each other's stretched out parts. I felt my own beat and touched my own soul.

The music shifts to a jazz riff. Staccato came out of my limbs in jerks and angles. "Get in touch with your anger," Kathy says, as the music builds to a jackhammer beat. "Feel the rage if it is there." I honestly don't have much anger in me. I'm not an angry person. But I experience a raw energy and I make it up. I feel it again and again in repeated thrusts till it is beauteous.

We move into Chaos. I descend into nothingness. There is nothing to grab onto, no grab bars or holds to keep me in place. I let myself dissolve into a cell blob on the floor, like a stem cell without a map or directions but that can convert to anything. Undone, I am ripe for becoming. I recast myself into spasms and throes of convulsions. Earthquakes I feel with my body shaking. I erupt in an explosion. My arms, my legs and my head burst out in all directions. I moan. My face is lost in the farrago and I collapse in a heap.

Slowly I lift my body and lighten my soul. I sweep myself up and become Lyrical. I am airborne, reaching to the sky. It is a flight of fancy. I am playful and have magical powers. I am winged as I fly around the room, arms outstretched to touch the stars.

Stillness is last. My energy goes inward. All my movements slow down. I've expended myself and I find the quiet within. I rest in silence, sitting on the floor, legs crossed, with my head bowed as in prayer.

I danced my dance. All the other dancers have danced their own dance. It is unbounded and spontaneous. It is what each of us makes it. Here in the moment is where I take it.

It is time to leave the hall. I feel fabulous with being so free! My emotions are loosened up and ripe for further exploration. Physically I am set at liberty. Joy is in my being.

Dear, dear Carl, you gave me a gift. Being alone has made me feel more free. When the chips are down, when push comes to shove, in the beginning or in the end, I have just me, no one else but me. Dancing my solo dance. I dove into my being and found a treasure trove of hidden expression and felicity.

Exhilarated after the dance, I met a friend over lunch at the Book Depot. My excitement was unrestrained in sharing with her the experience of the movement meditation. My body rippled and fluttered as we conversed about our lives.

I was raised a Baptist and Baptists don't dance, at least the Northern variety of Baptists don't dance. But I left that all behind in my college years. My first dancing was as a student at the University of Wisconsin in Madison. It started with square dancing and I was even a dance caller, as part of a course I took. The swinging in my partner's arms was dizzying but captivating. Not unlike the Sufi's spin which makes my head swim just to watch. "Allemande left with your left hand, DoSaDo," and "Acey Deucey" were delightful moves in the squares of eager dancers.

Social dancing was even more seducing. My first was the Union Ball. Chuck, my date, looked handsome in a tuxedo and I was resplendent in an aqua formal with skirt spread out in taffeta. He taught me the Samba and Jitterbug right on the dance floor. I liked to be in a guy's arms. It stirred up the sexual urges and we felt a mutual attraction.

That was before I met you, Carl. Once we met, we danced the

night away. You were raised in polka country in Wisconsin and boy could you do the polka. You taught me well and we were a pair. I can feel you right now moving me around with your strong long arms. When we danced the polka it felt like a very fast waltz with bounce and we nimbly swooshed across the floor. I loved to dance any dance with you. At the end of most dances you tipped me over in an arch almost to the floor. I would squeal with delight but it looked so elegant! With a slower sensuous two step, you held me closely, the crown of my head cradled in your neck. Time stood still and I wanted it to last forever.

My dear partner in dance and life, I wax romantic. But, how could I not stir with romance when I think of those times? You were the perfect mate. Two peas in a pod. Two kids on a swing. Two dancers in love we were. I wanted it to last forever but the forever could not be.

I returned to Tennessee Valley on another Thursday morning to let my body move me into dance. Jonathan was there to guide us. He laid his CDs in an order for playing on a small table, which also held the stacked amplifier and CD player. I did some yoga stretches to warm up my body while people trickled in. There were many familiar faces. In dance one can get on pretty intimate terms with another's form and visage. Your visual field is wide as you flit around the space and your eyes are open to just slip past other hands and toes. Your eyes meet and do a dance of their own.

I flowed right into love. I felt love throughout my body and mind. On my drive across the bridge to dance, the sun was glinting in a celestial glow on the copper red arch and spread to the water and hills ahead. I felt I was in heaven and love infused me.

My fingers touched the air gently. My arms reached out in compassion to souls in distress. My body swooped around in waves. Be kind to my knees I thought, as they flexed and extended with ease. Love my shifting feet because they support me and get me places. Give loving hugs to my strong torso for giving attachments to all my limbs. Devotedly I pet my chest and feel my heart and lungs working to support my life. I tilt my head and wrap it in my curving hands. My animus spreads love inward. My persona exudes loving kindness around me as I float around the room.

In staccato I jab elbows and knees into the air and toward another dancer who jabs the air toward me in return. We coil and recoil to spring again. Two others have joined us and we build to a frenzy. Heads jerk like marionettes on strings. Slowly the fire burns out and we move on.

Chaos takes over and I wander like a tippy canoe on shifting waters. I have no purpose and no goal in mind. Another lost soul catches my eye. We hunt for our way across the room and part ways on the other side.

I regain my senses by stretching my spine. My neck straightens up. My legs are planted to the ground. I am on solid footing and in good standing with the world. In Lyrical I am ready to skip and twirl around the floor.

How light I feel! The heaviness of the past is gone. My emotions seem protean in this milieu. They surface freely. Joy appears with surprise in my eyes. Happiness is in the air for the taking. My old friend sadness returns with a catch in my throat. "Hello friend," I whisper to the softening music. "I know you well. You can stay with me awhile." It is a many-sided emotional twirl I'm in. I take the sad with the glad. Anxiety shows itself with a hot surge in my arms. I have had my share of anxiety through the years but it is bigger now in grief. The mosaic of my emotional life is showing in broad relief.

I am ready for Stillness. My body and mind are heated and anticipating rest. The hardwood floor is my bed as I lie down on my side and curl in a 'C' looking for comfort.

Carl, you are my big 'C.' Please, circle your arms around my aching self and hug me tenderly. I want it now more than ever. Sometimes the solo dance in life is lonely.

There is soft ethereal music playing. The flutes could be on some distant star. Carl my love, do you have a heavenly offering for me, a needy soul?

"Ethel, you are beautiful in dance and in rest. Take heart in our devotion. Your loving kindness will restore you."

I came and left with love filling my being. Cars and people pervaded the roads and the bridge and I gave them smiles. I paid the toll taker twice the toll so that he could let the car behind me go through free. I took delight in imagining their surprise. I have given much kindness in my life as well as received it and now I had even more joy in the giving and fun in the doing.

I have been invited to a wedding! Tammy's close friends are getting married and they are my friends, too. It is outdoors of course since this is California. These two are launched on their careers and have found each other, as they said in their vows to share the rest of their lives with. Neither the bride nor the groom has been married before, noteworthy in these modern times.

How radiant and relaxed they are. I was a little nervous on my wedding day. She blooming in white walked up the grassy aisle, her dad at her side to meet her guy waiting in front of us expectant witnesses in white chairs. A soft guitar was playing as they met and smiled lovingly into each other's eyes. Young love, how sweet it is. They said their ceremonial words and kissed and then turned to smile at us. How happy we all were. But for some of us the joy was mixed with tears. I wasn't alone in dabbing my eyes. They say it is tears of happiness and perhaps that's true. But memories of young love return and of a whole life to follow, which is now in the past. That part is over and there come the tears.

Our wedding comes to mind. You, my husband to be in minutes, were young and handsome in a tuxedo with white jacket and black pants. I designed, cut and sewed my wedding gown. Yards of heavy white satin I bought from a fabric shop in San Francisco on Maiden Lane! I was a young unmarried maiden then. For two months I was an occupational therapy intern in this city and now it is my home again.

I carried my shiny riches back to my room at The Chalet in Pacific Heights and thought about you across the country in the Army Signal Corps. I longed for you but knew I would see you in a few months. There's no chance of that now, my friend no matter how much I pine. So, I'll stop yearning! Case closed. It's good to have a sense of humor.

The dancing has begun. The bride and groom are so gay. They waltz a duet around the dance floor so that we all can see them with their glow. Soon other couples join them. Dave is dancing with Melia on his shoulders. I decide to dance alone. The only solo dance around is mine. I am free! Unfettered and unconstrained. I dance my own waltz, winding through the couplings and gently swaying in time to the music. My head is high and my face is open to the world. I arch my arms up toward Melia as she and Dave swing by. She gives me a smile and makes happy sounds. From her high perch she can see a vista of moving heads. She spreads her glee to all as she leans and bobs her body, her precious little hands in a firm grip on Dave's crown.

Ah, to be the highest one. She is so young and small and yet she sees something we do not see. How happy she is. How wise she might be. If we saw through the eyes of a child what would we see? I am like a child skipping around the crowd, stepping over imaginary bumps, running to catch up to a figment of my imagination.

The dance is over and another will soon begin. I smile and laugh with people around me and soon the father of the bride asks for my hand. I am now part of a pair and he swings me away and pulls me back.

Holding my hand he turns his arm around my head and I twirl like a top and return to his guiding arms. How good it feels to be led. There are times in life for guidance and I am appreciating it now.

So often life is a balancing act. I like to be alone and I like to be with people. Too much of one or the other and I can feel out of sorts. I'm independent but sometimes I want help. I can twirl alone without restraint and still love to be held in someone's arms. Grief doesn't weigh me down too heavily because I have so much joy to balance out my sadness.

The just married kids are leaving. A whole life is ahead of them. Cupid and Eros, the Roman and the Greek, both gods of love have aimed for their hearts and left them swooning.

I returned on a Sunday morning to dance in meditation, this time at a high school gym in Sausalito. The weather is beautiful as usual. The sun is bright and the air is warm and light. Many people I now know in dance are arriving. The large door stays open and that is the feeling here. There is openness to all and everything. "Hi," "Hi," is in the air from everyone. "Hi," to Gary who leads the dance today. He is setting up the speakers in the corners of the room and gets our assist in managing the wire network. He sweeps the gym floor with a cloth broom as wide as I am high. The floor is ready and the music is on.

Gary has chosen "Persephone's Song" from "Luna." The strings are moving rapidly along the scale, first a violin and then a viola, an instrument I used to play. I flow right into the sybaritic sound, without effort in my tights and short knit shirt. I wore all white today. Is it the memory of the weddings? The one I just danced at and the one decades ago that was my own? Lying down in a swoop, I stretch my back on the floor. My hips roll. I hug my knees to my chest and move my feet in circles. I'm back up in a thrust. I let my arms and fingers spill into undulating waves, slipping through the group like an eel through water.

My spirit surfaces and somewhere in chaos I just stand and let go. I hear a woman's crystal clear voice singing through the speakers and rising to high notes. Her unhurried sound is supported by the deep-toned resonance of an organ, majestic and strong. I feel I am in a glass cathedral, exposed and so brave. It is a transcendent moment for me and I burst into tears. They come in a steady stream, wetting my cheeks and white shirt as I wipe my eyes with my sleeve. My throat is choked and my face is tight. My brows curl down and help release a flood of more tears. My chest is filled with sorrow and distress. I wrap myself in my arms, stroke myself lovingly and linger over my lips and my heart. I weep and whimper softly into my hands and my now sacred space.

Carl, I feel so alone. I have so much to bear. You left a gaping hole and I can't fill it. My heart is hurting and bursting. I have a painful knot to untangle. I miss you and want you and know I can't have you. Something's blocking my path to contentment. I could use some help to clear it away.

I am just barely moving in place. And within that space I let myself feel forlorn. The shadows of my heart magnify and disperse on the cathedral's reflective surface. There are no more tears to shed for now. My heart and body and mind are spent. In the quiet of my stillness I lie down and rest. I imagine a soft white puffy blanket enfolding me. An all white cloud I am, adrift on the floor, warm and safe and ready for healing.

Dozens of trips more I have made to the movement meditation. I have conversed with Carl's spirit whenever the spirit moves. He's illusive but when I reach him or he reaches me it is a gift. I have danced my prayers. I have put my psyche in motion and felt a waft of renewal. My wounds are healing. There is a renascence in the making.

One of my fond memories with you Carl is attending the dance in New York City. For years we were regulars at the Joyce Theater in Chelsea and the New York City Ballet in Lincoln Center. In the third tier with friends I was in seventh heaven watching the George Balanchine classics. So structured and precise was the ballet. The discipline and exactness of movement made for a beauty we recognized.

"Apollo" and "Agon" were regular fare. My favorite ballet was "A Midsummer Night's Dream." Mendelssohn wrote the music to the play that Shakespeare wrote. Balanchine choreographed it, inspired by the score. It is called a 'dream' because of the unrealistic happenings that occur to the characters. Puck weaves his magic spells throughout the enchanting story and dance. I like best when Titania awakens from a flower's spell. The flower has been pierced by Cupid's arrow for her to fall in love. When she sees Bottom, a weaver, whose head was transformed to that of an ass, she thinks him fair! I take it as a little lesson in seeing the beauty in unlikely people. You saw my joy, Carl, and felt it for yourself. You picked up on other people's happiness so easily and made it your own. I loved that about you.

Modern dance at the Joyce was creative and loose. We felt like we were dancing with the performers on the stage. I imagined taking leaps and turns in a contemporary way, while I was actually holding your hand Carl, in the seat next to me. You would almost skip across the streets afterward with a big smile on your face and I joined you, hand in hand.

So Carl, you understand my love for dancing my way and why I have found a home in action and movement. You have seen my pain come out until it's gone, at least for awhile. And I have felt your spirit move me. You are my invisible dance partner whispering in my ear sweet messages of love.

"I know what you mean. Happy dancing to you, honey."

CHAPTER 14
PLAY

Carl, in December 1995, a year before your death and before we had any idea that your cancer was looming on the landscape, you wrote to our friends and relatives, "On June 14th, Lauren was born to Randy and Bonnie, thrilling us all." We didn't meet her then, but all three came for a stay in our home when Lauren was nine months old. You and I fell in love with this little child.

Well, dear grandfather, she has been a restorative presence in my new life. Two months after you left your earthly plantings and when I found new plantings in California, I am seeing her again. I may have a broken heart but she touches my heart and the touching is so tender and sweet.

She walks but doesn't talk. You can see her almond eyes taking in all that is around her. We walk quietly hand in hand in my apartment to the deck and look out over the hills. I point out to her the trees, the rooftops, the airplanes and the birds and she looks and listens. We walk back in and nestle on the black leather sofa to look at a book. This child is an open book, ready and waiting for an imprint. What a remarkable phenomenon that is. There is so much clear space in her small personage to receive the world. I too have a clean slate for new discovery and perception. She is just beginning her life. Though I have lived a life, I am starting anew. Embarking on our trips to where we do not know, I feel I have a comrade, sailing off into the blue.

Like Lauren with no words on the tongue, there are no word imprints on the book I am holding, just pictures. We are looking at fruits. So colorful they are and with simple shapes a child can comprehend. Round like a ball and curved like a crescent moon. The primary colors, red and blue and yellow are next to purple and orange and green. Those colors are ours for the taking to fill in the shapes of our new lives.

The fruit on separate pages are a lemon, orange and banana and a bunch of grapes all round and purple. A delicious looking apple, a pear so green and blueberries spread out all in a row. All are ready to stir and arrange for a still-life painting of our own making. It is a moment in time like each of our moments together.

Lauren is ready for a snack and it is bread. We break our wheat bread slice together and sip our grape juice to quench our thirst. Simple foods she eats and I do too. And we both hunger and thirst for more of the new.

So soon, Randy is here to bring his daughter home. It is a spell we are in, my granddaughter and I of sweet tastes, pretty pictures, and warm embraces. We kiss goodbye and wave to each other's smiling faces and they go out my door.

Carl, it is a rich road I'm on, paved with gold, to have enchantment with a child. Dorothy's road to Oz was yellow brick and Heaven's streets are golden. Both are lands of wonder. What a good place it is to be in a childlike wonderment.

On another day, Randy took Lauren to our corner market and shopped for fresh produce, an abundance of which there is in this warm and sunny state. She chose a lemon as she usually does and said her first word, "lemon."

Randy dropped her off and we went down the back stairs to my garden. "Lemon" she said to herself, savoring the sound in her head and the feel to her tongue. We roam the spacious lawn. A sundial is in the center, open to make shadows of the sun. Flowers and trees are spread around. Small sculptures are nestled in spaces of fern. A clay figure in a yogic twist is sitting on the ground. I show Lauren my own version of 'the twist' and encourage her to try it but she is quiet and she just looks. A bisqued turtle beckons her instead and she sits on it slowly as a stately clay cat watches her warily from a nearby fern.

I settle into a corner of weathered gray wooden benches and small tables. Lauren sits with me but then ventures out on her own. She sees and breathes in the perfume of plum and apple and pear trees. Jasmine and honeysuckle, by the hot tub we never use, fill the senses. Fuchsia, foxglove and impatiens are lovely to look at. What a garden this is! Other flowers are in bloom, lower to the ground. Lauren gently touches the purple iris and bends down her tiny frame to reach the California poppy making an earth cover of gold.

We savor each moment. There is no space to grieve. We are in the moment now of feeling the breeze and watching the cat which is sidling the top of the fence. It is Lauren's cat! Black with a white heart on its chest. George has pounced through the neighborhood of fences, as only cats can do, and joined us, but at a distance. His mistress is pleased to see him and seems to understand his asocial stance. We sit and watch as he scurries away.

We lunch on bread and cheese and water right in the garden. The sun is near peak. I show Lauren the sundial with no shadow showing. Time is standing still. I feel no shadows in my life. We are both children now.

On a rainy day Bonnie came over with Lauren for the two of us to play. Lauren is saying more words now. "Hi Grandma," she says which pleases me. She has brought 'Dubbie' her well worn monkey and 'Bobacke' her cloth rabbit, names made up in her childlike mind. They join us in setting up two U-shaped footstools to inchworm through. We put the cream colored stools back to back to make one long tunnel and Lauren crawls under. "I can't see you. Where are you?" I call out till she wiggles to the other end with a grin. Dubbie and Bobacke are next and Lauren helps them with a push. I reach through and pull them out from the other side. We laugh for them because it was such fun. Her animals are jumping for joy in her little hands.

"Grandpa Carl and I made those footstools," I say. "We sawed and glued the wood together to make the shape of a 'U' and covered it with foam to make it soft. And then we covered the foam with suede cloth."

Lauren ran over to the refrigerator where a photo of the three of us is held with a magnet. Grandpa Carl and I are smiling and sitting on a sofa, holding nine month old Lauren on our laps.

"Grandpa Carl was a very special man and he loved you very much," I told her. She looked and listened and said, "I miss him." "I miss him too," I answered.

"Let's go to the park," I tell Lauren on another visit. And we are off down the hill. Past Jamba Juice, across the bumpy tracks on Judah and we stop in front of the Oriental Art Gallery, our favorite place along the way. There in the window are shelves and shelves of tiny figurines packed in to the hundreds. People and animals and made up creatures from every nursery rhyme, child's book and musical you can think of. We look at them in rapture as I crouch down to her level. Cinderella, Sleeping Beauty and the Wizard of Oz characters are just a few. Unicorns, rainbows and dogs all hold our fascination. It is hard to break away but we continue on past Park Chow Restaurant where we often eat, either the whole family or just Lauren and me, sitting on the counter stools to have garlic mashed potatoes and French fries with parmesan cheese. Across Lincoln Avenue we trip to the Arboretum in all its glory. The fountain is jetting high, the Asian men and women are doing Tai Chi, the baby turtles have grown. What joy we share! Back out of the park, we stop at the Produce Market for raspberries to eat later on my garden bench, a treat par excellence and home we go.

My piano is one of our favorite spots at home. I have a black ebony studio piano now, a gift of Carl's, instead of my big baby grand. Many times Lauren and I have sat there as I played and sang whatever her little heart desired. "Mary Had A Little Lamb" and "The Three Little Kittens," both verse after verse. The song we play most is "Over the Rainbow." I sing it clear like a crystal. Lauren sits close on the bench or off to the side on one of the cream colored stools, in rapt attention, with applause, and asks for it again and again.

You are with us, Carl. I can feel it. I don't talk to you out loud as I would alone, but we converse in my head. It doesn't send me into a torrent of tears. In my childlike mode with our granddaughter I feel happy and you compound the happiness. What a gift of a child we have wrought.

To become a child is so freeing and soothingly healing. I feel my heart mending with the play and the love. "I love you Grandma Ethel," Lauren says as she looks into my eyes. "I love you, too, Sweetheart," I answer with a hug.

Our second granddaughter, Melia, has just started walking and she sometimes joins our play. We play hide and seek in my apartment with no end in sight. "One, two, three," on up to 10 or 20 or whenever the scurrying feet become still, I count loudly from the kitchen or the deck, depending on the weather. I am on the hunt. "I'm coming, I'm coming," I call as I venture into or from the kitchen. I look behind the sofa and the soft chairs in the living room "Lauren is not squeezed into the book shelf. Melia is not attached to the ceiling," I call, teasing to perhaps evoke some muffled giggling. "I wonder where they are." Slowly through the rooms of the apartment I go - to the bathroom, my bedroom and closet, the small bedroom and finally the large room that looks out on the Golden Gate Bridge. "You are so well hidden I can't find you," I say as I open the closet doors and look in the corner. There are two heads low to the floor. "I found you!" I say excitedly. They squeal with delight.

We play this game endlessly. I am always the one to eventually call it off. I have only so much child energy in me!

There are days that I see just Melia and on one of those days my friend Mike called to tell me about the two beached whales on Ocean Beach that were on the news. Melia and I hopped on the N Judah to the end of the line and walked the rest of the way to the ocean. I could tell where they were by the stench. As soon as Melia saw the two large gray heaps, she clung to me, so I lifted her up and carried her to the water to see them up close. What I saw as amazing she saw as frightening and we backed away. My dear grandchild was in distress and I comforted her. Children want comfort. I have wanted comfort too and somehow giving her comfort gave me a comfort of my own.

Before Melia was born and about only four months into my grief, I comforted a soul mate cousin in distress. I wanted comfort almost desperately then. I felt so alone, even with having family and friends. The longing for Carl was so intense and I couldn't seem to lessen it. I found out that Noel was in the Fort Miley Veteran's Hospital in San

Francisco and that he was very depressed. His brother, also my cousin, living in the Midwest called me with the news and he was concerned. Of course I instantly said that I would go to be with Noel. I made many trips there, forty blocks away, and became his confidant. We walked around the grounds holding hands and I'd like to think that I was the kind of person with him that I wished for myself to aid in my own distress. I gave him time, a precious commodity these days. People are caught up in their own lives and do not seem to have time available for others. I listened openly to him, not fearfully with his fears, not 'oh how sad this is' but with gentleness and caring. I talked with him, accepted and did not judge him in any way, and I loved him. I gave him comfort and in some remarkable way it comforted me. Giving is the best way to receive.

He recovered, I think with his own mental energy, insights and panache. I drove him back to Mendocino to slowly resume his old life as a masterful gardener.

It was a godsend lesson for me to learn so early in my grief. Giving is the best way to receive. I have received so much from any kindness I have given and love I have shown.

Lauren and all my grandchildren, in their precious, childlike ways, have helped to soothe an injured heart.

One of many mornings, Lauren came over with her Dad, said goodbye and she and I were off to our amusements. Like Shakespeare said in A Midsummer Night's Dream, "How shall we beguile the lazy time, if not with some delight?" "Let's dance," she urged. Then, as we usually did, I made music at the piano and sang and moved my free body parts in time with the rhythm to get us juiced up. I joined her on the carpet, both of us humming and singing and laughing, and we clasped hands and danced. Moving our legs up and down and around, shifting our torsos and swinging our arms with sensual delight. Our dance takes us to the deck and we see the angel trumpet flowers on a large bush inviting us below. Down my green fungus covered stairs we step, past the hot tub on a landing where the trumpets were calling. We snatch a couple, put the large yellow bugles near to our mouths and our dance turns into a march, all around the green carpeted garden. We blow a vibrating tone that tickles our lips, as you do with waxed paper on a comb. We march past the large shrub of small white jasmine flowers and Lauren calls out "flower showers" as she brushes her small elegant hand against the branches and the tiny petals shower down. "Rest time," I call and we collapse on the bench and look around.

The plum tree is heavy with fruit and Lauren prances over and gathers up what has fallen. She arranges them in a purple circle on a low table in front of me. A circle as is in the fruit picture book, it is a simple shape a child can understand. But it also connotes so much good in our adult world, like unity, a circle of friends, a ring in marriage, coming full circle, and a circle dance. She tastes a ripe plum and consumes it and then another. Lemons aren't her only love.

We have come full circle back to my living room after our circle dance. "You were married," she says with a thoughtful look on her face. "Yes, we were married," I answer. "I wish he was here," she says. "I wish he was here, too. But he is in our hearts," I say pressing my hand to my breast.

The wonder never ceases. We indulge in awe and play and make believe. The world is simple and spontaneous. Unencumbered and free we are to do and be whatever and whoever we want to be.

Two more babies join our growing family. Isabella is born to Teri on the East Coast and Kai is born to Tammy on the West Coast. Seven grandchildren, God's perfect number. Isn't that perfect, Carl? Are you happy? Is happiness part of the spirit world? Or do you have just peace and tranquility?

Randy brought over a tent along with Lauren on a Saturday afternoon. He set up the red and blue dome on the wooden floor in the front bedroom and left a suitcase of toys and books. Then Dave came with Melia and her treasured toys and books in a satchel and sleeping bags under his arms. We girls are having a sleepover!

The girls set up their things in the tent and are ensconced for the rest of the day. I who usually join their play sit in the living room with a book and take in the sounds and the glory of the day.

"Are you hungry for supper?" I ask loudly from the kitchen. "Would you like to make carrot cake for our dessert?" "Yes, yes!" they squeal as they run to where I am. Whole-wheat carrot cake mix in a box with no sugar is what Lauren and I make often and now Melia will be part of the fun. They empty the box into a big stainless steel bowl and take turns adding honey and oil and egg and water. Kneeling on high stools to reach, they mix it up with a wooden spoon. The three of us work to pour it into my round tin pan and it is ready for the oven. While it bakes, we eat scrambled eggs and sliced oranges and sip seltzer water. "It tastes good, Grandma," Melia sweetly compliments me. The carrot cake is ready and both girls hold the handle of a metal 'Z' attached to the pan that slides under the cake to loosen it. They wind it round and round, it is such fun. I cut it into pie shaped pieces and we take our first bites. "Mmm, it tastes good. You girls did a good job," I praise them. "Thank you for making this delicious, healthful carrot cake." "You're welcome Grandma Ethel," they both answer politely.

After a night's sleep punctuated with a lot of whispers and giggles, they are up with the sun. I am up too and I suggest almost naughtily, "Let's go to the park and to the playground. There won't be anyone else there! We'll skip breakfast and eat when we get back." Eagerly we set off down the hill, through the park, past Kezar Stadium and to the playground. It is so early on this Sunday morning there is not a soul or sound around. The girls bound onto the jungle gym and the swings. They zip down the slides, intoxicated with the freedom and the choices.

Freeze this moment, dear God! A still-point in this magnificent span allotted to us on this earth.

The American artist Mary Cassatt's free impressionistic style paintings of mothers and children radiate happiness and closeness and love. Each painting shows just one second in time. I feel that second now and I want it to hold, like a painting. But the seconds have moved on to other seconds and now in another precious moment we are three picture-perfect happy, hungry kids, hand in hand, skipping along home.

A box of Annie's Whole Wheat Shells And Cheese awaits us on the counter and we work together eagerly to make our brunch and eat it gratefully. It is mid-morning and already it has been a full day. The Dads will soon pick you up dear children. This child will be left at home.

I plan to stay a child, Carl. It is the best way to go through life. Be like a child, Play like a child. Find delight in the simplest things. Love the flowers. Slide down the slides with spark. Swing on the swings with gusto. Climb on the jungle gym of life just to climb. Find friends who can be playmates. Believe in magic. Wish and dream.

Like Lauren and I sing at the piano: "Someday I'll wish upon a star and wake up where the clouds are far behind me...Where troubles melt like lemon drops away above the chimney tops that's where you'll find me...Somewhere over the rainbow, way up high."

CHAPTER 15
TRAVEL

"Honey, do you want to take a walk at the ocean? It is low tide and warm," Carl calls to me out of the blue. His spirit is alive and well!

Yes, let's! I answer and start off to the sea. I am caught up in the excitement of his being here and calling for me. It seems I'm always reaching for him, early on almost desperately, with no response. Now I'm more relaxed and I go with the flow.

It's in my neighborhood, I joke, knowing by now that part or the whole of him since death has seen me a hundred times or more on Ocean Beach in the Sunset District of San Francisco, my home.

"I have seen you many times," he gives nuance to my thoughts. "I feel your heart. It is lighter now. I'm so glad. You look wonderful too. So alive!"

We slipped through ripples and foam, taking in the glorious current of air.

"I love your quick step," he exudes. "You are as healthy and full of energy as ever. Will I be able to keep up with you?"

You jest, I know. You can keep up with anyone, I banter. Super power, spirit at breakneck speed, faster than light, Superman! Super Soul! How is it in your soulful world?

"Full of souls. It is hard to describe but it's where I am to be. I see your world and you, and then I am back to mine."

I see the sandpipers scurrying to catch the sand life exposed with the outgoing flow. The slanting light has caught my mind's eye and he is gone. I lost him with a moment's turn. The air is briefly still. He is back to his world and I to mine.

Stillness fills me. I am aware of every cell of my body imbued with life force. I am incredibly alive. It is as if someone turned up the voltage and I became a bioluminescent creature of the sea.

Yes Carl, my heart is lighter! And you have just helped, with our almost surreal conversation, to make it lighter still. Your humor is still intact. Whether your spirit is an aberration or an actuality you see that I am well and I see that you can see. I think you hear me, and do you see my surreal glow?

Dear Carl, traveler on another plane, I want to tell you about my travels. This first year after you flew away to your soulful world I haven't felt like flying across any oceans. Our seeking out new places together satiated me and I had no desire to explore the world alone. But as your spirit knows, I have flown in my home country from border to border.

Four times in a year I have flown to one of the places we used to live to be with Teri's family. My bonding with our North Carolina family is strong and I want to keep up a rich connection. We play and we laugh. Asher, not yet a teenager, shows me his meticulous hand-made charts covering centuries of you name it – all the elements and their properties, music composers, periods of natural history and Japan. Japan holds a special fascination for this young mind - its history and facts about emperors, samurai and geography. He draws from memory detailed maps of the whole world and I am drawn into his incredible world of the mind. Eric shows me his Lego constructions and dozens of origami creations. He draws spatial diagrams of geometric designs also from memory and I listen to his self-taught (just like me) piano playing. I marvel at both boys' capabilities and intense expression in their work and play. Isaac, a babe, is just beginning to learn through his five senses about our world.

I look at the 113D apartment building where we lived for just over a year and say out loud to myself and to you, Carl, we had such a good time here. I wish it could have been longer. I blow a kiss to the air and my eyes fill up with tears.

We all eat at the Golden Corral and save an empty chair for you. We remember that you would have loved the barbecue ribs. Every time that I pass Lowe's, my brain reflexively brings up a picture of the two of us hand in hand roaming every aisle for materials for our projects. There are business matters to attend to – I wonder what you would do differently in the decisions that I make. Teri and David and I talk on the big screen porch that you built, we thank you for making it and we make plans. There is an empty space in each of our lives, like the empty chair that we save for you, and we have such fond memories. After a week or two of family renewal I return to my California life.

All ten of us at the time remembered you in Wisconsin in the lilacs in the University Arboretum on our wedding anniversary day in May. Months later, dear Carl, husband and father and grandfather, I had installed a bench to honor you in the same Arboretum surrounded by lilacs. It is a pink marble free-form bench with a brass placard reading "In Loving Memory of Carl Radmer 1934-1997."

If your spirit is present like I feel it, you knew this at the time. When different family members have sat on your bench we feel so close to you. I have sat in semi-lotus in the rain on the pink marble with your own lotus in mind. Even dear little Melia, growing inside Tammy when we laid your ashes to rest, has climbed and stood on your bench. She's learning about you just as Isaac is learning from stories and photographs. It is an aural and pictorial history of you that we are passing on.

I drive up in my Volkswagen Golf to Mendocino to be with Noel on his isolated houseboat. We bushwhack through wilderness to get there. Wildcats have been here, too. I love the kerosene lamp light we read by, passed on from his father, my father's brother. We illuminate the past and talk about our dads, Arvid and Albert, long dead. Noel puts kindling and chopped wood in an old iron stove to keep us warm. In this isolation, like our fathers lived as young boys in Wisconsin cabin pioneer days, we keep the past alive.

What does it matter if we remember our dear ones of the past or not? Is it a sense of continuity we want? Do we feel a broadening of our awareness of ourselves? I think it makes us more complete to know what brought us to our birth. Melia and Isaac and all the rest know more about themselves when learning about people in the past that affected their lives. If one person's actions and choices can affect the whole universe, and I think it does like the ripple of a wave, then surely Carl's life impacts his progeny. I want them to know about you, dear Carl, so I tell them.

"Grandpa Carl could pilot a small plane," I tell Isaac as he tilts his toy plane up to soar and then dive. "I wish Grandpa Carl was here to give you ideas on how to attach those wheels," I say to Eric who is constructing a toy car out of wood in the workshop filled with Carl's tools. "He was so smart about putting things together." Eric finds his own way, I think partly because of what Asher's young mind years later brilliantly articulated, "What seems like a limitation (Carl's capability not here) is an inspiration." Eric remembered enough of Carl's skills and was inspired to use his own.

"Grandpa Carl loved his Birkenstock sandals," I say to the girls in San Francisco as they put their flowered sandals on to go outside. "He wore them all the time, even for hiking." Our daughter, Tammy, carries on the legacy and, as she says it, she practically lives in her Birkenstocks.

You are missed, remembered, honored, thought about, and loved. There are daily tributes in some fashion from us to you. I'd like to think that you know our every thoughtful gesture, though it serves us, not necessarily you. It makes us feel good to think about you and it assuages the sadness of your death. Part of you is still alive in all of us. And then there is your spirit hopefully alive and well in your spirit world!

I go to Phoenix to spend time with my long-time friend Jean and we roam the Phoenix Art Gallery to see a large collection of the colorful and strong paintings of Frida Kahlo. In 102° dry heat we float and chat in the sunny amorphous pool for hours and when we come out we evaporate so quickly that we shiver.

I fly to Cape Cod to have fun and good conversation with my friend Barbara. Her Winston died six months before my Carl died so we share a special bond besides our friendship. We remember with admiration both of you repairing a car in their driveway that was walled with several feet of snow. Barbara and I take turns pushing the heavy and partially dysfunctional grass rotary mower, cutting but not propelling forward, up and down the hills of her wide spread lawn. 'We are women! We are strong!' we sing out. But we admit it would be nice to have our men around.

I drive from the Cape to the Option Institute for a several day dose of happiness with old friends. Carl, the memorial fund I set up there in your name is such an honor to you. It is the perfect place for a tribute to you, such a radiant happy person you were.

It has been a year and a half and I am ready to venture out of the country without you for the first time since you died. I am flying to the South Pacific, Carl, uncharted islands for both of us – Moorea, Bora

Bora, and Tahiti. I am traveling alone.

Moorea is a heart-shaped jewel of an island from the small plane I am on. A beautiful mix of greens is spread out over the peaks and valleys of an ancient volcano. Shades of emerald green are flowing into the ocean of aquamarine and azurite blue, all gemstones, with white sandbars scattered close to shore. We land and a car takes me to the Beachcomber Resort. "You alone?" they ask me with puzzled looks on their faces. "You have only one suitcase?" they add looking at my small black suitcase on wheels. I travel small and light.

I have picked a strange place, not knowing it, to take my virginal trip. This is where the honeymooners go! I seem to be the only single tourist around. All I see are couples in the throes of love. It is about to hit me hard but I muster up all my happy beliefs to counter the strong urge to implode with sorrow. I do not want to be a piteous suffering woman in paradise!

I decide to be happy and to enjoy being by myself, even with the coupled world around me. The warm crystal clear ocean and the pool are always there for dipping. I am the only one in the aquascope under the water in the lagoon with the young French captain guiding the half-submarine craft from above. All alone I gaze through my fish bowl of a boat at schools of tropical fish, at octopus, tuna, eels, rays, sea turtles, and small shark. They come in an amazing array of colors. The large sharks are at lower depths but I might catch a hint of one below me. Is it a lemon shark? I bet it is 10 feet long and it is the intense color of lemon. I'll have to tell Lauren, lover of lemons. We surface and cute Captain Luc and I cozy up for a picture on top of the boat. I'm part of a couple now!

Quickly I'm by myself again and I eat in the restaurant spreading outdoors to the ocean. Young couples are all around, not a single soul in sight. I engage a few in conversation but they are all caught up in themselves and their lovers. I have a huge bed to myself under a thatched roof and Carl, it is hard not to want you.

A red 'Le Truck' is taking four others and me to the interior of the island. The volcanic peaks I saw from the air are jagged and the driver points out Moua Roa in the mist, 2500 feet high. James Michener dubbed it Bali Hai in his book and subsequent movie 'South Pacific.' We pass a pineapple plantation and stop for slices of the most succulent sweet pineapple spread out on a coconut palm frond. Hibiscus in red, white and blue stand out in the carpet of green that we pass along the road. Nature's miracles are so nourishing to my spirit.

Nature's magic comes in the form of dolphins, Melia's favorite animal. Another day, I am in the lagoon with the dolphins and a trainer. They are beauteous creatures arching in the air. A dolphin is resting in my arms. Though I almost feel like an intruder into his world, his eye connects with mine in a magical moment and I feel a bond of love. His eye is looking directly and gently into my soul. I am one of nature's beauteous creatures too.

There is a brief light rain and a rainbow arches across the island

and the sky. In this moment, my troubles melt like lemon drops and the clouds are far behind me.

A quick flight to Bora Bora, another volcanic island, and again I meet the puzzled looks and questions, "You alone?" "You alone?" Yes I am alone and resting in my roomy thatched bungalow for two. Where are you Carl? I have plenty of room for you. The bed is huge and the fruit basket is heaped. I'd love to share it with you. There is still room in my mending heart for your infusion of love.

A big catamaran takes a few people including me across the waters just before sunset. The air is warm and I hold my hand in the rippling water. It is so peaceful and calm and yet we are moving at a fast clip with our sails in an air space so large. It is like our planet spinning around the sun at incredible speed and we can't tell that we are moving at all.

Ukuleles are playing and Polynesian dancers in grass skirts are dancing in a line on the sand when we sail in and I go over to watch. The movements are so sensual and soon I am moving my own hips. You do not need a partner or a group for this dance and I am right at home in doing my dance alone. My body sways slowly and gracefully like the palm fronds and my hips swing in an erotic undulation like ocean waves. I am happy in my self-loving performance. I am sexual and complete. Who needs a partner? Ha! That would draw guffaws from this coupled young crowd of newlyweds. I was once enraptured with a man, both of us in love. Without Carl, I am smitten with life in every form it offers me. Life is good.

Another safari is in the offing and I go to the interior bush of ancient Bora Bora. It's a rough muddy rut of a road if you can call it that. The safari truck driver goes up the steepest of wet muddy hills. He defies the laws of gravity as we sit in the open back and remarkably we do not flip. Risk takers we are.

At a high point on our left and overlooking the island and ocean is an artillery installation from World War II, the cannon barrel aimed to sea but never used. It gives me pause. My older brother Dallas, a marine, fought in the 1940s in that war on Palilieu Island also in the South Pacific. He was shot at, took his risks and survived. A life could be defined as one risk following another, sun up to sundown. We're all risk takers whether we think so or not. And something always gets us in the end. Cancer got Carl. For myself, I want life to go on and on with no end in sight.

My trip is ending. When I came to the heart of French Polynesia, I didn't know that I would be challenging my growing equilibrium with immersion in Cupid's world. But I survived and happily so. I truly feel joy for all the lovers and happiness in my good fortune. I have a short stay in Tahiti and I am on my way home.

If you dig a hole through the center of the earth you get to China, I was told as a child. Though, in truth, directly under my feet in California is the Indian Ocean west of Australia and east of Madagascar according to Asher, my geography ace grandson.

My Aunt Mary was a missionary in China and as a child I saw the brocaded robes and slippers that she wore. China held a special fascination for me but I never stepped foot on this huge country until now. I am part of fifteen in a fitness group and we have warm and welcome entree to hospitals, schools, Universities and a few private homes in the cities as well as the historical and geological wonders in the rolling terrain of the countryside.

Carl, I could write a book about China, but I'll comment on just a few things. Builders that we were, if you were here, we could appreciate as a team the tenacity and skill of the army of Chinese people who built the Great Wall of China starting more than 2000 years ago through several dynasties. We would love together the grandeur of the architecture. I miss that partnership, dear friend. I climbed and walked on this gigantic dragon with another guy friend and imagined warding off the invading Huns from the North.

Come to Xian, Carl, and see the terra cotta warriors and horses and chariots. Like the Great Wall, they are more than 2000 years old. This underground mausoleum was discovered only thirty years ago. The life size figures, in the thousands, are in formation for battle at the beck and call of Emperor Qin Shi Huang, the first emperor of all China, in his afterlife. That they stayed hidden for so long is almost as amazing as the figures themselves. And how many more might be hidden elsewhere? And by the way, Carl, how is your afterlife? Is your spirit doing well?

My spirit is uplifted with the beauty of Guilin's candy-drop mounds of limestone along the Li River. We see double with the reflections in the clear waters, often portrayed in Chinese artworks.

One story, Carl, and I'll move on. From Beijing to Shanghai we have traveled and we are in a music class at a Chinese University, our group of fifteen standing behind all the pupils at desks. The professor clearly signaled to me to come to the front and play the piano. Now, I hadn't told anyone that I was a pianist, not the professor or my trip-mates. They told me later that they were surprised and impressed but assumed that it was planned. But it was out of the blue. I went to the front of the room and played "Whispering," short and sweet, from memory, with a large video camera rolling – perhaps for a private person or maybe for the news to all of China, for all I know. So appreciative the class was with smiles and clapping.

I remember you sweet Carl, in your last months, wanting me to play the piano. You seemed to be drinking the music in. I felt weepy inside with your ardor. And I felt such emotion with the playing - so heartfelt, so full of love for you, and so glad for your appreciation, but I'll admit it, underlain with an element of fear for the future. Thank you dear precious companion, accompaniment to my life and mine to yours, for all your loving attention.

Months after the warm welcome we felt in China, I daringly ventured to India. For days I was alone in Delhi except for the masses of people getting places and the bikhari begging for money. This is not a safe or healthful place. The sick, malnourished and crippled beggars surround you and touch you - I find my own way to experience it. Vehicular and pedestrian traffic is chaos – I become part of it. I could have put my hand in the little fencing the zoo afforded the white Bengal tiger and touched her – I stand several feet away from her gaze and admire her beauty. None of this is safe but I like it. The air pollution is heavy so I take shallow breaths. You take your risks.

In Agra, I joined a group with Deepak Chopra for a conference, "How to Know God." Carl you would have loved every part of this. We meditate morning and evening, do yoga and dance, eat regional vegetarian food, make trips to the Taj Mahal, and listen to Deepak impart words of wisdom. It is enriching in many ways. The Hindu religious leaders of India chant and impart their gods' blessings on us. We learn that the Hindu gods create, destroy, and create again. The Tibetan Buddhist monks take days to make a mandala, rich with color and design, and, after a day, destroy it in ceremony to show us the impermanence of things.

I know that subject well, Carl, and I'm still learning and adjusting to your impermanence. On some level I realize how arrogant it is for me to expect you to live beyond your allotted (whether by chance or by grand design) years. I still long for you but I think the strength of the yearning is lessening. I have such a full life.

At the end of a week a small group of us traveled throughout the state of Rajasthan with Deepak. We rode camels in the desert and elephants on the hills. We saw the pink city, Jaipur, and the blue city,

Jodhpur. A few of us spent an afternoon at the Osho Ashram at Pune, an oasis of cleanliness and Godliness. Every evening was a celebration of the Indian culture with costumes, dancing and food. I appreciate life in all its multiformity more than ever. Throughout we kept receiving pearls of dazzling thinking from Deepak. One night fireworks rained down on us, close enough to catch the embers as we danced jubilantly and sang "Hare Krishna."

Carl, you can find God, peace, joyfulness, and connectedness wherever you want. I found it everywhere. My travels alone are rich with learning and lucency and delight.

Around the planet I go, spinning on my axis like the polarity fields in Ayurvedic doshas. Balancing the forces – gravity, grief, and goodness. Getting more in balance in my body, mind, and spirit.

Carl, as I spin around the earth, where are you? If you aren't ubiquitous, at least you are fast moving. Is it possible that you are everywhere at the same moment, like God? A spirit mixing with other spirits is all part of the whole, which is everywhere.

Ah, for a traveler to be a spirit would be the height of exhilaration. I feel happiness and excitement with the thought of being even more alive!

Will you keep traveling with me, my co-spirit Carl? Wherever our co-pilot spirits lead?

CHAPTER 16
GUYS

Carl, you came to me in a dream. I had just moved to the West. I wanted desperately to reach you. A couple of friends, knowledgeable about dreams, thought that I might reach you in a dream. But I seldom remember my dreams. They suggested that before falling asleep in bed, I meditate on remembering my dreams. It is in the Theta brain wave state that we sleep and we dream. Theta is also associated with enhanced memory and integrative experiences. One morning in my pre-waking drowsy Alpha brain wave state, where relaxation and learning take place, the dream was there.

As the observer of the dream, I could see the back of me, sitting at a rectangular picnic table in the grassy back yard of a white house. An attractive man, whom I did not know in my awakened state, was seated across from me and we were talking. Carl, you were in your body off to the right side. I felt your presence and your demeanor and your thoughts. You were apart from us because you were not directly part of my life now. You emanated beauty and love. I had a strong sense of you and you told me, "It is okay to enjoy the company of other men." You were such a kind and thoughtful man that it fit that you would give me such a generous gift and so soon after you died.

In Theta state, what you voiced brought together any conflicted feelings that I might have. Your acceptance became part of a larger whole for me in living my life. In Alpha state, I learned what I already knew intuitively about you – that you were fine with any way I wanted to experience my time on this earth. Granted, I didn't need your permission, but if I knew you didn't like something I was doing, it might get in the way of my happiness. Knowing what your spirit sentiments of affirmation were, kept my psyche at peace.

When I plunged into life in San Francisco I was open and friendly to all. Even in my sadness, I extended myself to guys and gals of all ages and races. I wanted friendship and people with whom to have good conversation. I would talk with guys, almost as an exercise, to keep my social muscles from atrophying. It was important to me to stay comfortable with men.

In a crowd of people I mixed as freely as I would have in my married days. I ventured with some daring to speak with anyone who didn't look threatening or who didn't look walled off with his or her attachment to someone else. I am a social being and I want to have good talk and discourse. My urges were not for romance, though I realized that perhaps somewhere down the line I might feel such inclinations. Friendliness and possible friendship led me in my social encounters. They still do.

My consciousness was different, though, from when I had you Carl as a mate. Now, I noticed who was single if it was obvious, though, I still don't necessarily notice wedding rings. I was aware of possessiveness shown by a woman to a man, when I, obviously alone, approached them. I noticed the looks of disinterest or perhaps lack of courage on the part of men to talk with me.

In my single state, I found my friendships with other single women to be more precarious and tenuous. A close friend stopped calling me when she met a guy whom she started dating. When she stopped seeing him she started calling me as if nothing had ever happened between us. At a social gathering, women friends, looking for a man, would drop me if a possible man was around. As an unattached single myself, I was competition for other single women. Women would cancel a planned get together with me if a guy came into their lives. I made myself available in friendship to women to discuss their problems with men and, when they connected with a guy, I did not hear from them until it was over, or ever again.

I found myself operating in unfamiliar territory. I thought I had left the whims and insecurities of teenage-hood behind. I did not like this kind of behavior and did not emulate it. I really made an effort to stay in touch with women friends, throughout my marriage and in my new life without you, Carl. I took myself out of anything that others were seeing as social competition. I made overtures to men on my own terms for friendship and did not drop my other friends in the process.

A telling contrast to my disappointments with women in competition for men was hanging out with my men friends or alone in coffee shops in the Castro or at the Castro Theater and striking up conversations with the fun, mostly gay men around me. We were not in competition for or threatening to each others' friends. I loved my lesbian friends also. We could be totally ourselves, often outrageous and not be playing these silly games that I was experiencing in the heterosexual marketplace.

I wanted good friendship first and foremost. As I approached my one-year mark of singleness, I felt more ready to let a friendship spill over into romance. More than a year after your death, Carl, I went alone to my first singles dance. One can find singles dances in almost any publication, poster or by word of mouth in any part of the country.

I braved it first in North Carolina on one of my longer visits with Teri's family. I met an attractive man – he approached me – and we connected. Now I've certainly had this happen before in my daily life but I kept it at a friendship level. This time it led to romance. And he was romantic. He brought me flowers, gave me special attentions that I hadn't had since you left this earth, and it was lovely. The sex came naturally and he was a good, considerate, and exciting lover. We stayed in touch when I returned to San Francisco, on the phone and fax, and I saw him on return visits. But he didn't match my wants for someone to keep in my life. I broke it off when I was with him in person so he wasn't left wondering with silence on my part.

That experience told me that I did like having a man in my life for romance, but by no means was it essential. I wanted to meet other men and I searched out singles groups. There is a bunch in the San

Francisco Bay area, besides singles dances. The first I joined was "Table for Six."

My status is that I am in my early sixties and young and vital. Age in years does not matter to me for myself or in what I look for in others. Attitude and spirit do matter. And it was with that attitude that I approached singles groups and meeting guys and gals.

"Table for Six" arranged a table gathering for six people, three men and three women, in any of many restaurants on one of several days that I was available in a week. I did meet men and women over the years in this group. I engaged in a lot of interesting and fun conversation with dozens of people. I dated some of the men. A rare few might have led to romance. I met a couple of terrific women who are still my friends. One of the women said to me over lunch, and I concurred, "The best thing that happened in that group was meeting you." The other good friend and I got together every week with our two grandchildren and she and I went to many events together for years.

Almost concurrent with joining "Table for Six," I joined "Great Expectations." Profiles and photographs in books, alphabetized by first name, and videos, mine included, fill the shelves of the center. I pored through books of guys for maybe an hour or two out of a month - I had only so much energy for this. I made contacts with some men and they made contact with me and we would meet. I dated several good men, a couple of them invited me to their homes, were very hospitable and we had nice conversation, and then I lost interest. They didn't have enough of something for me, maybe a little bit of charm or pizzazz. I met at least one man that led to romance. He was tall, handsome, charming, and successful. He massaged my neck while sitting over lunch at the Raw Food Restaurant. We vacationed together on a weekend. We talked about relationships and I said if ever anyone didn't want me I didn't want him either. Well, that happened. He lost interest and I did too. Carl, I talked with you about that, because I felt puzzled and a little pained. You helped me get through it.

Churches have singles groups and I partook of one, "The Lafayette Singles." This group is so popular that hundreds show up on a Sunday evening for a program and socializing. I briefly dated a few men, but nothing much came of it.

Carl, where are you, I have wondered. I'm not expecting or looking for a carbon copy of you. I'm sure it doesn't exist. I am deliberately open to all kinds of people. But I do want some basics in a companion. Kindness, intelligence, a light side - call it humor, and not too much baggage.

Not with men in mind but just for the fun of it, I had photographs taken and I signed with a casting agency to be an extra in advertisements and television and movies. What a kick! I was background or a 'fuzzy' as they are called, at least once for all three – ads, TV, and movies. On a movie set with Robin Williams, I sat at a table in the background, my face made up and my hair styled extravagantly, and wearing a spectacular gown for a party scene under the dome of City Hall. Filming went on through the night. In the waiting between takes on the set, a young, handsome actor who was a 'waiter' introduced himself to me. He called me days later and we started seeing each other. I wasn't sure what his intentions were but I liked his company and he mine. He was black which I found alluring. We played jazz together at the piano, sang, and had an appetite to do new things. I surprised myself and let it become physical. The intimacy with him was exciting, adventurous, and very satisfying. Age and color do not matter! We got together occasionally and still do, maybe once in a year. Without even discussing it, we seem to agree it is not a full, long-term commitment.

Thanks to a friend, Donna, I played with the Internet off and on for a year until I became tired of it. We sat in her apartment, up the hill from the Trans America Building still towering above us, while she helped register me for Match.com. This is a world of unknowns, cyber-sex innuendo, and after clearing through the maze and muddle, eventually meeting some nice people. I did date some men whom I met on-line, in the flesh. One was a pilot. Tim and I flew directly over San Francisco Airport in his small plane and this place of action looked absolutely still and silent below us. We flew all over the area taking in the majesty of ocean and broad landscape. He talked about our flying way up the coast for a weekend. We went to the opera and we walked with his dog on the ocean below where the hang gliders fly. We were fine together but he decided that his heart was with another woman, among over a hundred women he told me were interested in him.

I do meet people by chance. Occasionally I meet a man in the course of my day – on the MUNI, at the library, or at a gathering - and we like each other enough to do things together. Rarely has it gone beyond friendship.

One afternoon, Lauren, nearly five years old, and I sat at the counter at Park Chow Restaurant. We were having our usual French fries with parmesan cheese for Lauren and garlic mashed potatoes for me. A man sat down a couple of stools from me and we started talking. I included Lauren in on the conversation and we kept it up until I felt it was time to leave and we said our goodbyes. When outside, Lauren sweetly said to me, "Maybe, he could be your husband?"

Ah, if life were that simple. Meet someone, as easily as sitting at a counter, talk, and get married. Life is more complex and in limbo for me. I'm not sure I even want another husband. The searching I've done for friendship and romance among the male population is not always very satisfying. Sometimes, I feel that I am not cut out for all the work. There are pleasures along the way but I tire of the effort. I wish I could have more of what I had before, with you, Carl.

But the reality is what I make it. Life without you is different now. Other people grace my days. I get as much pleasure as possible out of everything that I choose. By chance, maybe I'll meet some man and by choice, have pleasure in his company. Or perchance, I'll stay alone.

CHAPTER 17
ALONE

Early one weekday morning, sunny and warm, I walked through the park, past the Shakespeare Gardens and the outdoor Music Concourse to the Japanese Tea Garden. The Tea Garden gates were open and the gatekeeper wouldn't arrive for another hour. This hospitable city graciously opens the gates of the Tea Garden for free in the early morning, before the crowds come and before requiring an entrance fee. As I entered the main gate to the spacious gardens, usually filled with people, I knew that I would be wholly alone.

The garden is lush with green. I walked to the left around the drum bridge and skittered across the water on deeply-set black stepping stones. Ahead of me is a koi pond. Alone, I circle the water on the 'sprinkled hail-stone pavement,' with a bamboo railing to catch hold of, but I am sure footed. I glimpse two crane sculptures, standing tall above the water. I, too, feel poised above calm waters.

Stone lanterns are scattered throughout the garden to light my solitary path. Around the bend of koi ponds and dwarf trees I go, taking in the beauty of the red and black pines, much loved by the Japanese. Black pine is a masculine symbol and the red is feminine. They are shaped and trimmed by gardeners and then sculpted by the elements into intricate, beautiful shapes. I have weathered the storm and have been sculpted into a changed form of myself, as elegant as the red pines.

Up the stairs is the Temple Gate in red, white, and green and higher still, the red pagoda, overlooking all below. I imagine being the only one on earth, alone like the pagoda on the hill.

More paths I take, past the Lantern of Peace (a gift of the children of Japan), and onward to the Zen Garden. A garden is considered to be one of the highest art forms in Japan. This garden has a miniature mountain scene. A green island, off center, is surrounded by a gravel river and a stone waterfall. I meditate on being alone, not on what I am missing, but on what and who I am. I am complete and whole.

My path steps up to the large, bronze Buddha, his right elbow bent with the flat palm of his hand facing me, as if to say "Peace" and "Blessings." It is my nourishment. I dine alone. The long rustic curved bridge takes me to the quiet Tea House and just around the bend is a wide slope of grass and a bench at the base for resting. I am exhilarated and do not need to rest.

The gate is in view and I am still all alone. I have covered every path and, as I knew it would be, there was not another person in this garden on my journey. I hear the leaves of a thousand cherry blossom trees fluttering in the breeze, a grace note to my flow. In Japan a few of these same trees live to the felicitous number of a thousand years of age. I am young! I am serene and strong, completely by myself. I pass through the gate, go down the wide stairs, and return to the peopled world.

At noon, I meet my friends, Harold and Joan, for lunch at a restaurant in Pacific Heights. We hug and kiss and make our selections of healthful fare from the menu reflecting the California scene. Then I break my news. "I have just had a singular experience!" I exult. "Early this morning, I walked all through the Japanese Tea Garden without another soul around. I was absolutely alone." They joyously become part of my excitement. "It was remarkable!"

To be alone is to be completely by oneself. Inside and outside the Japanese Tea Garden, I was and am alone. I admit it. I honor it. I praise it. I am alone. I live alone.

I am not married. I do not have a helpmate or helpmeet. I do not have a steady lover. I do not have someone I can count on all the time or who has time for me like a spouse. I do not have a partner who is always available and always kind. I do not have a man with whom I am in love. I do not have a steady, fully compatible, committed friend. I do not have a companion with whom to share my life. I do not have the easy excitement and fun of available physical intimacy. There is no dear one present from sun up to sun down and through the night that cares about my thoughts and fears. I do not have a man, whom I treasure, for me to give and do all of these things in kind. I am not those things and I do not have those things.

What I am is single. Single as in a singularity which is remarkable and unique and I am remarkable too. Astrophysicists consider a singularity to be a hypothetical point in space. Mathematicians call it a point in a complex function that is undefined. 'Hypothetical' and 'undefined' applied to my single state give me wide birth to define my state of 'only one.'

But I first need to clear my head of what society thinks. Single-hood is not always well thought of. People often consider it a less desirable state than to be coupled. Single people themselves tend to think of it as second best.

Gender and age can be vulnerable to biased thinking. Single men are more in demand that single women in the dating market and are consequently viewed more positively. A single guy at any age is called an eligible bachelor. His image projects freedom, excitement, and power to do what he pleases. He can stay single and be well thought of and even envied by other guys for his being single. A single gal is available and looking and the clock is ticking in terms of her attractiveness and appeal. She is more likely than a guy to be viewed in a negative way in her singleness. As the years tick by, people might see her even more negatively – pathetic, desperate, lonely.

We attach more importance to the need for a woman to find a man than we do for a man to find a woman An older guy is still in demand, even if he is not actively searching or has not taken good care of himself. An older gal is much less in demand and works harder to find a guy. She has more of a challenge to be happy in single-hood, because the culture does not support her to be happy and content alone. We are caught up in this system and it is hard to break free. We buy into this thinking instead of trying to change it or just be what we want to be.

I propose that we think apart from men and women who live by the culture's prevailing views. Carl, you know that I have always been an independent thinker, so you are not surprised with what I am saying to other sojourners on this earth. Let's not believe any of the things we are told about ourselves. Let's do what we want and get what we want. Single-ness can be a happy state unto itself and does not have to be dependent on couple-hood. Let's define being single and alone in a way that suits us.

Alone is single, solitary, and separate. Single is separate, distinct, and unique and also unmarried. The Latin 'singularus' translates via Old French as 'Alone of its kind.' In all of humankind or any 'kind' grouping, of which I am a part, I am apart and alone. We have things in common – being part of the human race – and we each are unique and one of a kind and absolutely alone.

Being single, I am free to be and do whatever I wish, with no attachments, compromises, limitations, or accountability. I have absolute freedom. Satisfactions are in my grasp. Happiness I can make for myself. I am the creator of every event in my day.

It is a great state to be in. I can choose to not have and to not look for a partner and be perfectly happy alone. I can satisfy myself sexually if I desire it or find someone I really like and am attracted to, but who does not suit me as a full-time life partner, if I want intimacy. I can look anywhere for company if I want it in anything that I do. But alone might be better – it's my choice. I can hike, see a movie, attend a talk or concert at my whim. When traveling alone, the culture and the people might be more accessible to me than if I were attached to someone. Plus I have the freedom to be spontaneous and change a plan.

What's to stop you from going it alone? Does the stigma of society make you uncomfortable or does your own lack of confidence get in the way? Let it go! Do you think it would be better to have a mate with whom to share the experience? It doesn't have to be better or worse - just different, when you are alone.

Define your own life, I say.

Emily Dickenson, the American poet, was a recluse, an extreme form of being alone. Early in her life she did share intellectual interests with a couple of men. She was determined to remain unmarried and subservient to no man and answerable to no one. Then, in her mid-twenties she slowly started retreating to the confines of her family homestead and her own consciousness. She wrote letters and poetry in her bedroom until her death at age 64 years. Fortunately for us, she wrote over 1,700 beautiful, intimate poems in her solitude.

Mary Cassatt, the impressionist painter, born in 1844, with an independent streak for the time, often painted women alone in their activities – a woman sitting alone in a private box in "At the Opera," and a woman drinking tea alone. Mary knew at age 16 that she would be an artist and would not devote herself to a husband. She never married, though she and Edgar Degas were lifelong friends. She said herself,

"Oh, I am independent. I can live alone and I love to work." And she did that to age 82. Her friend Degas said, "…to be a serious artist…one must constantly immerse oneself in solitude."

I love the image of women alone. To be alone in all its glory – to travel, eat and sleep and climb. A woman sits by herself sipping tea in a delicate porcelain cup in a French café, patrons watching from distant seats, as they watched the woman alone in the private box in Cassatt's "At the Opera." A single woman, perhaps me, is lost in the 'grand theater of her mind' at Emily Dickenson's small writing desk in her bedroom in Amherst.

And I see Julia, feeling on top of the world, in Somerset Maughm's novella, "Theatre," and the movie "Julia," after her acting triumph on stage. "I've decided not to join the party," she said. "I want to dine alone tonight." And she dined alone at the Berkeley at a table for one. "I shall never in all my life have another moment like this. I'm not going to share it with anyone."

To be by oneself is good. We deserve it, we bask in it and we thrive on it. And if we are not used to it, we can grow into it. I am complete in myself, my dear, I say to whoever is listening.

Are you listening, Carl? I think that you are. You have seen me grow into it. I have come a long way with you and without you.

On the day that you died and my first night without you, all of our children and I slept in the same house. We needed the comfort of each other nearby. On my second night I returned to our apartment to sleep in our big bed alone. As I lay there on 'my' side, bereft without you next to me, I turned on the radio – something we did not do together in respect for the other's sleep - to soft classical music. I will take pleasure in listening to music in bed, I thought, in this one moment of time. I will feel at peace for as many moments as my mind can hold. And as the hours and days go by, I will let that peace and pleasure grow.

Well, Carl, the peace and pleasure are bigger now, just as your spirit told me would happen when I sat on the rock, my eyes wet with tears, conversing with you on Pescadero Beach. I'm alone, Carl. Just like the Buddha says. I have solitude in the silence. I feel joy in the quietness. What do you think, Carl?

"I am proud of you, beyond words. I love you deeply. Have dinner alone in your favorite place and I'll join you and we can talk about old times. Be happy and well, kindred spirit. In spirit, you're not alone."

CHAPTER 18
REFLECTIONS

Was the sky trying to tell us something? It was the August before you died. We took the motor boat out to the middle of the big lake at our summer place in the Northeast. Carl, you turned off the motor and you and I sat close on the bow of the boat, and our friends, Vinson and Mary, sat on cushioned seats in the stern. The sun had just set and the sky was erupting in an incredible display. The four of us saw shapes filling the sky that looked, in cosmic terms, like an allegorical epigraph of archetypal objects, all represented in an intense coral color. We were stunned into silence. We had never seen anything like it. Vinson said later that it looked like the work of a magician, or God, or some other power. We felt like we were being talked to but we didn't know what was being said.

If someone had a cosmic message, for us we didn't get it. We said that it seemed like a symbolic representation of something, we knew not what. Barely a week later, Carl, you and I learned that you had cancer.

You and I took down the art exhibit of my glass sculptures at the Page Walker Gallery in North Carolina the first of August, just two weeks before we saw the writing in the sky. As we loaded up the car - bless you dear heart for your help in all parts of my art endeavor - I said,

"I think this is my swan song, Carl." It turned out to be my swan song in more ways than one and it was your swan song as well.

After we learned that you had cancer, a friend suggested that we see Sonia, a spiritualist. We were in the throes of your threatening death and we searched for anything that might help us, guide us, and give us knowledge and comfort. We made a couple of visits to Sonia. She went into a trance-like state and spoke of all your wonderful qualities, which was true, and called you an old soul. She said that you would live and write a book about your experiences to help others. After you died, I visited her again. She described your physical state at your death in a way that was not true. I thought how wrong she was on several counts. Now, I think she might have been right in a way about writing the book. You and I have been in conversation since your death and you are speaking with me now as I write the book.

I talked with you at least once after your death about your goodness and my appreciating it and wishing I had appreciated you even more than I did. Here was your answer. "If you had died before me, I would have wished, too, that I had appreciated you more than I did."

Carl, I feel your presence now. I am reading in a soft chair with light streaming in the windows. You are doing the same in a neighboring chair and you let yourself doze. I resist my sleepy feeling. That reminds me, Carl, of times in our past life, when I might urge us on to some project, when I saw you nodding. Please forgive me for not always respecting your quiet retreat.

"You did do that sometimes, but there was usually good reason. It's ok."

Respectful of the caught-in-time stillness, I whisper. Thank you Carl, I love your being here. Thank you for being with me.

I think part of your spirit resides in me. Soon after you died, I started waking up in the middle of the night and staying awake, just like you used to do and I rarely did. You loved pears and would share a slice with me - a slice was enough. When you left the earth, I started eating entire pears with pleasure and I still do. I eat more butter like you always did – I used to eat almost none. I began eating your multi-grain flakes which I seldom did when you were alive to eat them. I became more patient with things that I used to be impatient with and you would be patient about. You hear accounts of people who have transplanted organs and take on traits of the deceased person from whom the organ came, not knowing that the person had those traits. I feel as though that happened with me, though I knew your traits, and that I have taken on some of your habits and characteristics.

Carl, my dear mate on our life's journey, you were a buffer to my world with its hurts. When I felt injured or irritated with someone's behavior you always helped me put it in perspective. "Do you really want to feel that way?" you in the flesh would ask. And now when arrows have hit, my wise one, you in spirit answer me in such a clear way, in my tears.

"Don't try to change the bad. The bad will change itself. Be what you are. Be kind and not angry with anyone. You are kind and nice to all. I am in your heart. I'll always be. It will be a long time before you pass on. Enjoy and be totally at peace. You are at peace now. Let others do what they do. I wrap my arms around you, surround you, around you. I love you."

I'm sitting in my living room now, in my green swivel chair, my eyes closed and I feel your spirit with me. I am crying and we are sharing our love in a beautiful way. I am moved to go through the five senses in a kind of meditation with you.

Taste comes first. I can still taste the Spanish rice and malted milkshakes you used to make for our family on Sunday nights. I taste the salty perspiration of your skin on a warm day as I hold and lift your swinging arm on a walk and bring it to my lips.

I can smell your skin and your beard after a shower, as if it just happened now, so fresh and moist and clean is your body. I can smell the sawdust that spun out from your band saw when you were cutting lengths of board for so many construction projects.

Seeing is believing. I believe you are beautiful as I look into your beautiful face looking at me and meeting my eyes. I look at your whole gorgeous body and see the long, well toned arms and legs and the hairs on your firm chest. I believe you are strong and in good shape.

"I love you," is coming from the library in your sweet happy voice as I call out a bye and love you as I was leaving the apartment in

North Carolina on an errand. "I'm done," you say with satisfaction as you lay down your latest book on the table in the evening and we both head for bed. I hear all the silence we had together. We didn't need to talk. We relished the sound of quiet in our being together.

Feeling your hands, your beautiful hands, is my cachet of support and comfort in shaky times. Your left hand is in my right hand as we walk together and your right hand is in my left as we sit by each other at a concert or movie. I feel your palm so strongly in mine and I feel it staying there. "I'll always have my hand in yours," you touchingly say to me now.

Sensing you through five channels of impression and excitation should be enough, but I still ask you to show me in a direct physical 'out-of-the-way' way that you exist now and I will surrender to believing. But a knock on the wall or a flashing of lights is not there. I'll choose to be content with your words and spirit presence and to believe in your messages apprising and advising and loving me. They are real enough.

These tidings from you, among many, are all real. Four years after your spirit passed on, you spoke to me at one o'clock in the morning in my bed – I wrote it down - on an occasion of my awakening and reflecting on your death.

"I didn't want to leave you. I had to be almost forced out. I wanted to stay with you. Now, I can say it is good that I'm here – at spirit level – learning and growing. You were a reason. My death was a gift to you. I wanted you to have time by yourself – to do things you wanted to have done without me there."

Carl, it's true. Like you are saying on your spirit level, I have grown in my earthly form in ways that I never would have grown. I have had the experience of being alone. I am enjoying life in a different way. I'm exploring who I really am and what I can be. I have found peace and happiness without you.

A year and a half after your passing, a dear New York friend, Maura, came to stay with me for a visit. We had a dialogue together, exploring her desires, and in the process I had my own moment of awareness. "I got it!" I said, after she thanked me for the dialogue. I realized that I had found peace and happiness and that I am ok with your death and that you would want that for me and be glad. Granted, that eureka, light-bulb moment hasn't held for me 24 hours a day or through the weeks and months. But that awareness has stayed with me on some level and has grown and become integrated with all my parts and is a much larger part of the whole than it used to be.

I have learned that we are all ultimately alone. We start out alone in the womb. We end up alone in our death. In between, which is our life, is ours alone for the taking.

I look on every experience as a singular experience. It is what I make it and I don't necessarily expect or long for more. I have learned more than ever to take my pleasure in the moment, with or without people, and to not feel an urgency or distress about the moment to come. We don't have to make a connection. We don't have to meet again. Let it flow and life flows along more gloriously.

I know now that in looking to be whole, I don't want to look for or need someone to fill a hole in my life. In my early days of meeting guys, I was sometimes distressed and perplexed with their behavior and way of being. In the Denver airport, waiting for a plane to meet a friend in Vail, I conversed with you, my other half of our whole, about what was going on with me about guys. That might seem weird to some but it was a natural for me since you were no longer my earthly partner and your understanding and wise spirit was and still is a presence in my life.

"Keep doing what you are doing," you offered. "You will get what you want." I learned in my living that I can be utterly content, tranquil in my aloneness, and serene, and at the same time be open to a man coming into my life. "Just be open to it," you said. My self-found guide is to find rather than seek.

Your death propelled me into another life for myself. It is impossible that life could be the same. I have found that I am not a victim of your death, but rather a shaker and mover with new opportunities.

I can have fun without you. A half year after you died, my friend, Annie, and I had a vegetarian dinner out and then went to the 'Heart and Soul Jazz Club.' I didn't need you. We had a banter that I love, listening to the mediocre jazz trio with guitar, bass and drums. "They're playing yet again in the same key!" I say to my friend. "Don't they know how to stretch their imagination?" "The bass is plucking the same notes on the string and the drummer is off-beat," Annie whispers. "Let's take off on our own beat," I suggest while chuckling, as we walk out the door. Weeks later, we again make fun for ourselves and go to San Anselmo for a Constance Demby live new age music 'only in California' happening in Demby's multi-faceted home. The sofas, candles, art objects and icons, and meandering spaces are fit for a movie set which in fact her music is – a live version of her soundtracks to films.

The fun has taken over more of my 'living space' since then and I have fun when I want it. I don't have to have you, Carl. I don't have to be with anyone. I can make my own fun or share it, if the urge is there, with strangers or friends.

I think I'm a better person, Carl, without you. Not that I wouldn't want you back. I still would want you back in a heartbeat. Just the other day, on our forty-seventh wedding anniversary, I visited your memorial bench in Wisconsin with Asher. The lilacs were in full bloom with their sweet aroma. Purple and white, just like on our sweet wedding day. "I still miss your Grandpa Carl," I told Asher. "I do too," he said with longing.

By 'better,' I mean that I'm really evaluating and evolving my behavior in a clearer fashion. I honestly think that I am more deeply loving. I have a stronger realization of what I want and one thing is to give to others. I do it more freely and spontaneously and joyously. I phone friends. I lavish kind attention. I look people in their eyes and listen with caring. I try to be fully present. I am happier, and that is better for me and others around me.

I am more taken with life than ever. My family holds my love in even greater increments. I appreciate all the forms that a living thing takes. I'm in awe of the variety and tenacity and beauty of life.

Ilya Prigogine, Nobel Prize winner in chemistry in 1977, was also a student of philosophy, which influenced his research. Prigogine always emphasized that it is out of chaos, turmoil, and disorder that higher levels of order and wisdom emerge. Psychological suffering, he said, can lead to new emotional and spiritual strengths. I think that happened with me. I know that I have evolved from the upheaval of your death, Carl. My broken pieces have been put together, but in a new way. I seem more able to enjoy the energies passing through. I go with the flow, I enjoy an inner state of flow, and I flow, with grace, from one moment to the next.

Philosophically, I don't know the purpose or meaning of life. The Dalai Lama says the purpose in our living is to be happy. I would say it is not our purpose unless we want it to be and make it so. You are the scriptwriter of your own play. You are the author of your own story. You are the artist of your own creation. You can make it up. The energy of life is just dancing and I can make up my life in a dance. I can make my time here fun. I can fill it with anxiety and regret or I can be happy and serene.

I do think everything in the universe, as physicists say, is connected in a matrix of energy and matter. Each thing affects everything else. So we are one with everything. The unfolding of the universe is happening in its own way and is guided by something way bigger than me. Maybe it was an intelligence that created the writing in the sky or maybe a confluence of chance events. Whatever it is and whatever the universe holds in its hands, I am going along for the ride. I can ripple and dance and soar and that is what I am doing.

After my first gaze at the gliders from my small plane in the sky over San Francisco, I made many trips to Fort Funston to watch the hang-gliders fly. So brave each person was, fit into their sock of a glider, to run and jump off the cliff to catch the wind. I imagined myself doing it hundreds of times. One day I went to another windy site on the Bay and strapped myself to an open glider with a small motor and a pilot nestled in, still a brave thing for me to do, and we flew off across the water. We hung onto the struts of the wings and he steered and gave me a turn to steer. We banked and we sailed all over the Bay. People we could barely see, standing on a ferry boat, waved up to us and we waved back. The bridges stretched across the Bay. The city's buildings were thrusting from the ground below us.

I did it, Carl! My dear love forever 'til I die and join you in the sky or wherever you reside, did you see me? I felt that you did. I soared to new heights, above where the eagles fly. It is a metaphor, as I suggested when I first saw the gliders, for my play, for my unwritten script, for my life adventure without you.

I am freely flying now to new places. I am floating in the wind, head on with courage. I am weaving high over the challenges of rippling waters. I dare to sail into the unknown. I feel light and strong. I am spreading my wings.